W9-CRD-598

INTERVIEWS WITH JESUS

INTERVIEWS
WITH
JESUS

JERRY VINES

BROADMAN PRESS
Nashville, Tennessee

© Copyright 1981 • Broadman Press
All rights reserved
4251-80
ISBN: 0-8054-5180-3

Dewey Decimal Classification: 240
Subject headings: DEVOTIONAL LITERATURE//
JESUS CHRIST—TEACHINGS
Library of Congress Catalog Card Number: 80-69241
Printed in the United States of America

Contents

1.
An Average Man

John 1:35-42

This series will enable us to see how the Lord Jesus Christ dealt with various individuals. We realize that Jesus sometime related to people on a mass basis as he addressed himself to the multitudes. There were times when Jesus, the great teacher and preacher, would speak to people by the thousands and would meet their needs through that kind of communication.

But it thrills me to notice that Jesus singled out individuals. Sometimes Jesus would talk with one woman. At times he would converse with one man. At other times Jesus would be interested in one boy or one girl. Some of the greatest truths Jesus ever taught were shared with one individual—for instance, it was to one man that Jesus said, "Ye must be born again." It was to one woman that Jesus said, "God is a spirit, and they that worship him must worship him in spirit and in truth." It is marvelous to view our Lord in the Gospels as he dealt with individuals on a one-to-one basis.

In John 2:24-25 there is a rather intriguing statement about the ministry of our Lord with individuals. Read these two verses and see how Jesus dealt with individuals. "But Jesus did not commit himself unto them because he knew all men, and needed not that any should testify of man, for he knew what was in man."

Here we have a statement about the knowledge of our Lord concerning the hearts and lives of individuals. First of all, we are told that Jesus understands the constitution of persons. He knows all people. This means he knows how people function. He knows what makes humans tick.

Our Lord knew that people have a physical nature, so Jesus talked about their physical needs. He said, "Your Father knows that you have need of all these things. . . . Seek ye first the kingdom of God, and his righteousness, and all of these things will be added unto you."

From time to time Jesus healed people who had physical diseases. Jesus Christ in that instance is the great physician.

But Jesus also knew that people have an emotional nature, that they have feelings, and Jesus understood the mechanics of the human personality. The psychiatrists of our day are trying to discover truth about the human personality and how persons are structured emotionally. Our Lord who was man—but was also God of very God—understood how people were put together.

On one occasion when Jesus was dealing with Simon Peter, Simon said to him, "Lord, thou knowest all things." That is, Jesus knew the heart of people. Jesus understood what man is, how he is constituted emotionally. Jesus proved himself to be the "great psychiatrist." Jesus also understood that humans have spiritual natures. Jesus was aware there was something about a person that was not physical and not merely mental. There was a quality about humanity that was deeply spiritual in nature.

As Jesus dealt with individuals he went to the deepest levels of their lives and addressed himself to their spiritual needs. Somehow we seem to have forgotten that man is a spiritual being, that man is not only body, mind, and emotion, but that man is also a spiritual being. In the average university today we build a stadium to care for at least 50,000 people, ministering to physical needs. We build classrooms to care for 5,000 to care for their mental needs, and then we build a chapel of about 500 to care for their spiritual needs. Somehow we have forgotten the fact that man is a spiritual being, but Jesus didn't forget. He was the great preacher who could talk to people about heaven and hell. He could talk to them about eternity and what life is really all about.

The Scriptures say that Jesus knew all people. The Bible declares that he knew what was in man. The Bible tells us that Jesus understood man's condition. Jesus could look into the hearts of individuals, and he could recognize what was there. We are going to consider various interviews of our Lord, and we are going to discover that he dealt with each person on an individual basis with his set of circumstances and his particular needs in mind. There were certain overriding, broad principles which were true about the condition of every person with whom Jesus talked.

Now there are two things that Jesus understood about the condition of persons. Number one, he understood that mankind is sinful. Jesus said in Luke 11:13, "If ye being evil know how to give good gifts unto your children. . . ." In that statement Jesus makes a comment about the basic condition of man's heart. Man is a sinner, man is in need of a Savior. Jesus simply put into words what psychoanalysis today has discovered and has put into different terminology. Freud and all of the others who have opened the door for psychoanalysis have proved that there is something basically wrong with the inner core of persons. Someone said there is a great deal of similarity between a psychoanalyst and a coal miner, except the psychoanalyst goes down deeper, stays down longer, and comes up filthier. Man is basically a sinner; man is sinful in his heart.

Not only did Jesus recognize that a man is sinful, but he also understood that man by condition is savable. There were no impossible cases with our Lord. There was no one beyond the realm of the saving grace of the Lord Jesus Christ. In our day we have people we call "incorrigible." We claim they are beyond the help of anyone, but Jesus Christ looked at people and saw them, not as they were, but as they could become by His power and grace.

I heard about an old-timer who was listening to his young pastor preach on original sin. After that sermon the old-timer said, "Well, if we're really all as bad off as that, then God help us!" What the man was saying is exactly what has to be done. God must help mankind, and that is why Jesus Christ came into this world, and that is why Jesus dealt with individual persons, for it is only when Jesus Christ lays hold of one's life, one is savable and redeemable. A few years ago I was talking to a young man who was in tremendous trouble. I was trying to help him and point him to Christ. I noticed there was a tatoo on his arm. The tatoo said: "born to raise hell." I said, "Young man, you are not born to raise hell. That is not why you are in this world. You are not in this world to cause all the trouble you can cause and to mess up your life as badly as you can mess it up. You were born to find Jesus as your Savior. You were born to have your life transformed by God's miracle-working power."

So Jesus saw the condition of men. He saw them as sinful, but he also saw them savable—and he changed their lives. He could take a Simon Peter and make a mighty preacher out of him. He could take a sinful woman and make a faithful servant out of her. Jesus dealt with individuals.

Now let's look at this individual we have read about in John 1. I call him "an average man." In verse 40 we are told the name of this man. He was one of the two who followed Jesus from John the Baptist. His name was Andrew. The name *Andrew* means "manly," and I think what we have here is indeed a manly man. But he was also an average man, a rather ordinary kind of man, and that is of considerable encouragement to me. Some of the Bible characters I could never be. I could never be a Simon Peter and preach a Pentecostal sermon. I could never be a King David and write a beautiful song. I could never be an apostle Paul and write a book of Romans. I cannot be those kinds of Bible characters, but when I read about this man Andrew, and discover that he was an ordinary man who was chosen by Jesus to be one of His followers, it makes me rejoice.

I think we have a wrong idea today. I somehow feel we have the idea that, in order to serve the Lord Jesus Christ, somehow we have got to be spectacular and sensational. We think that before we can adequately testify for the Lord, we have to be an All-American, or a beauty queen. But Andrew dispels that myth altogether. Insofar as we know Andrew never preached a sermon. So far as we can tell he never wrote a book. So far as we know his life personally never influenced the masses of the people, and yet Christ saw something in Andrew which caused the Lord to spend some time on a one-to-one basis with him.

There are three things I want to write about Andrew. One, I want to notice his possessions. We find it in verse 41 of this chapter. Andrew told his brother Simon, "We have found the Messiah. The word for found there is closely akin to *eureka*, meaning, "I have found it!" Andrew was saying here, "I have made a marvelous discovery. I have found something I have been looking for all my life.'' Andrew had found the most precious treasure any person can ever find. Andrew had made the discovery which changes time and also changes eternity. He had discovered the Lord Jesus Christ precious as his own personal Savior.

Now as we look at this possession which came to be Andrew's, we discover three facts about it. First of all, we notice his *search*. In verse 35 there is the story of John the Baptist on the banks of the river Jordan, and Jesus Christ showed up to be baptized. John pointed to Jesus and said, "Behold the Lamb of God." Then those two disciples turned and started following the Lord Jesus. One of them was Andrew, and as they were following Jesus, Jesus turned around and looked at them. He asked, "What seek ye?" The word *seek* there is a most interesting word. It means a quest for something that is hidden or lost, and it reveals what Jesus saw in the life of Andrew. For the most part Andrew spent his time fishing. That was his occupation. But he had heard about John who was preaching at the Jordan. He left his fishing for a few days and had gone there to hear John preach. When John pointed to Jesus, Andrew began to follow Jesus. In essence Jesus was asking, "What is your search in life?"

That is one of the deepest questions anybody could ever ask you. I would ask you that question now, sir. What are you seeking? What are you looking for in life, young lady? What is the purpose of your life? What are you searching for in life? Everybody is searching for something. Everybody is on a search. Everybody is on a quest for something. Psychiatrists relate that there are four things people are basically searching for. They are trying to discover how to be useful in life. Two, they are trying to discover how to get rid of guilt. Three, they are trying to discover how to love. Four, they are searching for a feeling of security.

What is your search? What are you looking for in life? Jesus speaks to your heart as he spoke to the heart of Andrew. That question really hit Andrew, for Andrew responded in verse 38. He asked, "Master, where do you live?" It's as if Andrew were saying to Jesus, "You have asked me a question that plumbs the very depths of my being. Lord, you have asked me a question that is so close to my life that no short period of time can do. Where do you live, Lord. Let's sit down, and I want to talk this thing over with you."

As we see his search we also see his *satisfaction*. After he had that time with the Lord Jesus Christ he came to a satisfying experience with Jesus in his life. Jesus said to Andrew, "Come," and literally He said, "you shall see." Jesus was making a tremendous claim. "You come after me, Andrew, and you will find what you are seeking." I pick up this word *seek*, and I follow it in the life of Jesus, and I am amazed at how many times Jesus used that word. For instance, Jesus said, "Seek and ye shall find." He said, "Seek ye first the kingdom of God." So when Andrew came seeking Jesus, he made the marvelous discovery that Jesus had also been seeking him. Jesus can satisfy what you are looking for. I don't know what it is. I don't know what the deepest need of your heart is, but Jesus does. He looks at your life, and he says, "You come to me, and you shall see."

I heard Jeannette Clift George talking about looking for her car keys in her purse. She said she was looking for her car keys in her purse casually. Then she said she started looking for her car keys interestedly, and then diligently, then desperately, and finally frantically. And she said, "You know what. My car keys weren't in my purse—I was looking for my car keys in the wrong purse." Some of you are frantic, some of you and are diligently and frantically searching for the meaning of life, but the problem is you are looking for the meaning of life in the wrong purse. You are looking in the wrong places.

Jesus speaks to you today. "Come and you shall see." So Andrew came to Jesus Christ, and he was satisfied he had found his Messiah.

Now I want you to notice his service. Turn to Matthew 4. I want us to look at a little passage which tells how Jesus called Andrew to serve Him. See Matthew 4:18. On this occasion Andrew had gone back to his fishing, and Jesus had not yet called him to follow Him. After some period of time when Jesus first met Andrew, Jesus was walking by the Sea of Galilee, and saw Simon Peter and Andrew his brother as they were casting a net into the sea. Jesus said to

Andrew, "Follow me and I will make you fishers of men." Andrew just forsook his net and followed Jesus Christ. When you find the Lord Jesus Christ you find something to do—you find a place of service.

Up to this point he had been fishing for fish, but Jesus expanded the horizons of Andrew. Jesus said to him, Andrew, if you will come after me I will give your life an eternal dimension, and I will give you a reason and purpose to live for. You follow me and I will make you a fisher of men.

Now this average man had more than prominence, more than prosperity, more than many famous people today. This man had found the Messiah, and the Messiah had given him something to do, his possession.

There is another thought about Andrew. I want you to see his position. Have you noticed the position that Andrew has in the Scriptures? Look at John 1:4 and see. The Bible says that one of those who followed him in the streets was Andrew, Simon Peter's brother. Did you know that's just about the way Andrew is described everytime he is mentioned in the Bible. Almost without exception it is always "Andrew, Simon Peter's brother." He seems to have had a secondary position in life. He seems always to have been in the shadow of his more famous brother. He seems always to have been in second place. In fact, when you look at the list of the disciples you will discover that he is never any higher than number four on the list. You will discover that he was not in the "inner circle" of the Lord Jesus. He was not on the Mount of Transfiguration with the other three. He seems to have had a rather ordinary, mundane position.

When I study the life of this ordinary man I seem to get the idea that Andrew had learned some secrets about his position in life. I want to speak about your position in life, and if you will listen to them, heed them, and live by them, you will never again be discontented or unhappy about your place in life. I think he had learned three basic secrets about his position.

He had learned the secret of capacity. He had simply learned what his abilities were and was willing to use those abilities as he served the Lord Jesus Christ. Over in Romans 12:3 it says that we are not to think of ourselves more highly than we ought to think, but every man should think soberly, according as God has dealt to every man the measure of faith. We all don't have the same capacity. We can't do the same things, but the secret is for us to learn what we can do, dedicate it to the Lord Jesus Christ, and just let Jesus use us in that position.

The Bible talks about the church as the body of Christ. It is compared to a body, and in your body you have fingers, and they have a capacity. You have eyes, and they have a capacity. You have a big toe, but you know that big toe is not too attractive, and it's rather unimportant, it seems. But you stump it, and you'll think you are all big toe! Let something happen to that big toe, and try to walk. You can't do well without a big toe. And in the body of Christ, regardless of what your position may be, you have a capacity and that capacity can be useful in the work of Christ. Have you learned the secret of capacity just to be what you can to the glory of God.

Two, he had also learned the secret, not only of capacity, but the secret of contentment. There is no evidence that Andrew was dissatisfied with his position in life, or that Andrew was ever discontented with where the Lord Jesus Christ had placed him. He was contented to be where Jesus wanted him to be. Now many of you are not contented. Some of you are tall, and you wish you were short. Some of you are short, and you say, "Oh, I wish I were tall." Some of you are skinny, and you wish you were bigger. Some of you are bigger, and you wish you were smaller. It's hard for us to be content where we are, isn't it? If you really want Jesus Christ to use your life, then you should make up your mind that wherever he has placed you in life is because of his divine plan, his love, and his omnipotence over your life. Just be happy and contented to be where Jesus wants you to be!

I heard a little legend about the plants in a garden. A man was walking through the garden and saw a little pine tree, and the little pine tree was all drooped over and sad. The man said, "Little pine tree, what is wrong with you? The pine tree answered, "Oh, do you see that mighty oak? Its branches lift to the sky. Its leaves blow in the wind. Oh, I wish I were a mighty oak tree." Such a sad, little pine tree!

The man walked over a little further, and he saw a jonquil all drooped over and sad. "What's the matter with you, jonquil?" "Oh, do you see that beautiful rose? Folks are all the time coming by and smelling its beautiful aroma, and I'm just a little jonquil. Oh, I wish I were a gorgeous rose."

Then the man went by a little violet, and that little violet was as bright and cheerful and happy as it could be. The man said, "Little violet, why are you so happy?" The little violet said, "Well, you know I just figured if the Lord had wanted a mighty oak tree he would have planted one, and if the Lord had wanted a gorgeous rose, he would have planted it, but evidently my Lord wanted a little violet. So he planted me, and so I'm going to be the brightest, happiest, most cheerful violet I can possibly be." Listen, friends, learn the secret of contentment. Learn that wherever Jesus has placed you in life is where he wants you to be and he has a purpose.

Here is the third secret. He learned the secret of *constraint*. Paul declared, "The love of Christ constraineth us." The love of Jesus Christ compels us to love him and be what he wants us to be, wherever he wants us to be. Your contentment or discontentment with where you are in life and your position in life is a commentary on your love or your lack of love for the Lord Jesus Christ. Are you just willing to love Christ right where you are to serve him right where you are. Here is his position. Second fiddle if that be, Simon Peter's brother if that is how it is to be, but Andrew was an average man who was used by Jesus Christ in the position where he was. His possession—he had found the Savior; his position, he was where God wanted him to be serving to his capacity, but now I want you to see his passion.

Here was a man who had a passion in life. There was a passion that ruled and motivated Andrew unbelievably. You remember the Lord said to Andrew, "Follow me and I will make you fishers of men." From that point on Andrew became a fisher of men, and everytime you see Andrew in the book of John he is introducing people to Jesus. He had became an introducer. I have the idea that anybody who finds Jesus as their Savior will automatically become an introducer. I don't think you can know the Lord Jesus Christ and not somehow have a desire to tell someone else about your Lord. Brother, if you are not fishing you are not following.

In this first chapter he introduces a brother to Jesus. Look at verse 41: "He first findeth his own brother." He simply went out there and found his brother. He did that first. He put priority on introducing a brother to Jesus Christ. I am amazed how individual Christians can get so messed up in their priorities and put soul-winning at a secondary place in their life. I am amazed at how churches can become involved in peripheral matters and leave out the main business of telling people about Jesus Christ.

I could take a whole platform of bottles and think how to fill up those bottles with water. I could use a bucket full of water, and I could pour that water over those bottles. I would get some water in the bottles, but the best way to fill up those bottles would be to do it one by one. Preaching is kind of like pouring the bucket over the bottles. But there is nothing that will improve on one-on-one winning of people to Jesus. I was pastor of a certain church for about four years. Through most of that time there was a high school boy who came to our services. I thought he was a member because he was more faithful than most of our members were. One Sunday afternoon I went by his house, and casually mentioned Jesus to him. To my utter amazement I discovered that he had never been saved. In five minutes I showed him the gospel plan on salvation. He received Jesus as his Savior! What I had been unable to do in four years of preaching to that boy, in five minutes I did, talking to him one on one. Friend, I can win some folks to the Lord in the pulpit, but you can win many people on a one-on-one basis that may never be won to Christ through the public preaching of the gospel.

Andrew put it first. And I want you to notice that he went to a difficult place. Where is the first place he went? He found a brother. The hardest place for you to bear a witness is at home. Do you know why that's true? Your family knows you. They see all the warts, all the inconsistencies. They know you exactly as you are.

Peter was a pretty tough guy to witness to. He had been known to "cuss" you out. I can see him now. Andrew, an ordinary kind of man, goes home, and there sits rough and rugged Simon Peter. "Simon, I've got something I want to tell you." "What do you want to say, baby brother?"

This reminds me of one night when I was out visiting. I was going to an unsaved man. I knocked on the door, the door opened, and "Man Mountain McGoon" came to the door. He looked down on me and bellowed "What do you want?" I started to say, "I'm selling brushes—wrong house!" I could feel my courage easing out of my toenails, but I was amazed how the Holy Spirit took that big man and melted him. And Simon Peter, that big, rough, rugged fisherman was tamed. Andrew said, "Listen, Simon, I want to tell you we have found him. We have found the Messiah." And the Bbile said "he brought him to Jesus." Ah, the greatest thing you can do for another person is to bring him personally to Jesus Christ.

Andrew introduced a brother to Jesus. That was the greatest day's work Andrew ever did. Don't you imagine Andrew rejoiced on the day of Pentecost, even though he was on the sidelines somewhere, and there stood Simon Peter preaching the gospel. Three thousand souls were saved, and Simon Peter became the spiritual father of those three thousand! But Andrew was the spiritual *grandfather* of those three thousand!

Ah, yes, Simon could move a multitude, but Andrew could move Simon. You might move some Simon if you would introduce him to Jesus.

Now turn to John chapter 6. He not only brought a brother to Jesus—he brought a boy to Jesus. I love this chapter in John. It's the story of Jesus' feeding the 5,000. They were all gathered there, and it was about noontime. Jesus (in verse 5) said to one of the other disciples, "Philip, where are we going to buy bread that these may eat?" Jesus knew what was going to be done. He was simply checking out Philip, and Philip flunked completely (verse 7). Philip said that two hundred pennyworth of bread was not sufficient. Today he might have said, "Lord, we could buy all the Big Macs they have in all the stores, and still could not feed this crowd." In verse 8, "Andrew, Simon Peter's brother, saith unto him, there is a lad here." The boy had five pieces of bread and two fish, so Andrew introduced him to Jesus. Andrew was the kind of man who saw potential in a mere boy.

Listen, don't you ever underestimate the value of winning one precious child to Jesus Christ. D. L. Moody, the great evangelist, was preaching one night. When he came home his wife asked, What kind of results did you have?"

He replied, "We had two-and-a-half converts."

"Oh, you mean you had two adults and one child."

"No, we had two children and one adult!"

Oh, some of you people Sunday after Sunday teach boys and girls in Sunday School, and you may feel they don't get anything you are trying to teach. Maybe they are unruly and mischievous, but who knows who's sitting in your Sunday School class. Maybe a Billy Graham sitting in that class, a William Wallace, a Lottie Moon. Andrew saw the potential of Jesus Christ in the life of a boy. Andrew became a living link between a lad and the Lord, and he led him to Jesus Christ. You can do that. Introduce someone to Jesus.

The third time Andrew appears is in John 12, and it is close to the time of the cross. In verse 20 we are told that some Greeks came to Jesus. In verse 21 they went to Phillip and requested, "Sir, we would see Jesus." Here were men who came from a land of philosophy and religion, and yet they were dissatisfied and searching in their hearts. Philip went and told Andrew, and what an appropriate choice, for Andrew had been on the same search. He knew what it was to search for meaning in life. Andrew and Philip (verse 22) told Jesus. They brought the Greeks to Jesus.

There is a world out there crying, "We would see Jesus." There is a world out here that is saying, "I don't care about your fancy church. I don't care about your big program. I don't care about your prestige. I don't care about your prominence. We would see Jesus."

If you cannot preach like Peter, if you cannot pray like Paul, you can tell the love of Jesus, and how he died for all. You may not be a David. You may not be a Paul, but everyone of you can be an average Andrew.

2.
The Man Who Became a Rock

John 1:41-42

The most prominent man in the ministry of the Lord Jesus was Simon Peter. The Gospels say more about this man than any other disciple, and Simon Peter has more to say than anyone else who came in contact with our Savior.

I believe most of you would have liked Simon Peter. I have in mind that Simon Peter was a big, rugged kind of man. He was outgoing, outspoken, and the kind of big guy you might have liked to be around. Personality analysts would claim that his personality was "sanguine." That is, he was outgoing, he was enthusiastic, and he was very boisterous. Whatever Simon did he always did it with a flair. If it was a success I will assure you he "knocked the top out." If it was a failure it was a big one, for whatever Simon did he always did in a big way.

Now there is one word that seems to summarize what this man Simon Peter was when the Lord Jesus Christ met him. I think the word is impetuous. I see that he was impetuous in his words. In fact, Simon Peter was always the one who seemed to give the answer. He didn't think normally before he talked. He just opened up his mouth and whatever was there came out.

Recall the time when Simon Peter was with James and John on the mountain of transfiguration, and the Lord was transfigured before them. Simon Peter said, "Lord, it is good for us to be here," and Mark adds in his Gospel that Peter spoke these words because he didn't know what to say. That's the way he was, impetuous in his words.

And also he was impetuous in his ways. He moved quickly. He acted, and after it was all over, if he got into trouble, he regretted it—but he didn't seem to mind jumping into things. For instance, I see him impetuously cutting off the ear of the high priest's servant. I see him impetuously running into the empty tomb of our Lord and then running out again. He was headstrong, but also flighty, in his ways.

He was also impetuous in his worship. Whatever else we are going to learn about Simon Peter we are going to realize that this man really loved Lord Jesus Christ, and so it didn't matter if he had to swim through the water or walk on top of the water. Whatever it took Simon Peter wanted to be at the feet of Jesus. I suppose you will probably think of a fellow Christian who will fill the bill of Simon Peter. Many Christians are like Simon Peter. Many are gung ho and impetuous.

There is something about Simon Peter you always like. He is one of those guys that makes you scratch your head and ask, "What in the world do I see in that guy?" Yet, when you are with him, you can't explain why you overlook all of the things about him that irritate you and you just love him anyhow. Simon Peter is the man whom Jesus Christ transformed into a rock. I want us to look at our Lord as he interviews Simon Peter in successive interviews, and I want us to see what Jesus Christ did in the life of Simon Peter.

First, the Lord *captured* him. The Lord captured him by the promise which He gave to him. The Scripture declares in verse 42 that when Jesus beheld him, he said, "Thou art Simon, son of Jona." The word beheld there is quite an interesting word. It means to look in, and it carries the idea of penetrating an individual. It's not a glance, but it is a gaze. It's looking into the very depths of a person. Jesus looked into the very heart and core of Peter's being and said to him, "Your name is Simon, but it is going to be called *Cephas*," or a stone. I find that captivating and interesting.

We know, of course, that the Bible teaches Jesus is a stone, a rock. In 1 Peter 2:4 and following Simon Peter himself called the Lord Jesus Christ a living stone. Jesus is the stone upon which we build our lives. Jesus Christ is that rock upon whom we can depend. I appreciate the hymn, "Rock of Ages, Cleft for Me." It was written by Dr. A. M. Toplady. The way God spoke to his heart about that song is rather interesting. He was walking one evening through a valley between two cliffs, and a great storm came up. The lightning crackled from cliff to cliff, and the rain began to pelt the rocks. So Toplady climbed up one of the cliffs, found a cleft in the rock, and hid himself there until the storm passed over. God spoke to his heart and told him that is the way the Lord Jesus is. "Rock of Ages, cleft for me, Let me hide myself in thee. Let the water and the blood, from thy wounded side which flowed, rock of ages, cleft for me, let me hide myself in thee." And those who know the Lord Jesus have found that indeed he is a rock on whom we can depend. He is a rock on whom we can build our lives.

The Lord said something to Simon that absolutely captured his life. The Lord looked into the life of Simon and said, "You shall be called Cephas, or Peter, which means a stone." I think that must have astonished Simon Peter. This is one of the few occasions in Simon Peter's life when he was speechless. He didn't respond. He didn't speak at all. Do you know why? I believe that in his heart, Simon Peter was so astonished that it left him speechless. For in his heart, Simon Peter knew that if there was anything he was not, it was a rock. He was more like the shifting sands on the Sea of Galilee. There was virtually no strength in him, but there was weakness. He was so vascillating. He was so impulsive. He was so little of what Jesus Christ predicted he would be. Christ has a way of doing that, doesn't he. Jesus has a way of looking beyond things as they seem. Jesus has a way of coming to our lives and saying, "I'm going to make something out of you."

There are many instances in the Bible where names are changed. There was something about changing of a name that indicated a change in the character of the individual. People change names today, and it may not necessarily mean that. I heard about a fellow who went before the judge to have his name changed and the judge said, "Well, young man, what's your name. The fellow replied, "William Stinks, sir," and the judge laughed. The judge said, "Well, I don't blame you, ole boy, with a name like that. I would get it changed, too. What do you want it changed to?

"Bill Stinks, sir."

Not much change in character there, but when Jesus Christ took charge he saw something in a life that could transform that life. You will be amazed what Jesus can do if you will allow your life to be captured by him. Why, you give Jesus a crabapple, and he will give you back a golden delicious; you give Jesus a reed shaken in the wind, and he will give back to you a mighty oak withstanding the storm. Give Jesus a Jacob, and he will give you back an Israel; give Jesus a Saul of Tarsus, persecuting the Christians, and he will give back to you a Paul, mighty preacher of the gospel.

Listen, you give Jesus a sinner marred by the fall, and he will give you back a saint polished like a palace. Give Jesus you *the way you are*, and he will give you back the way you ought to be.

Simon Peter thought in his heart, *if this man Jesus has that kind of confidence in me and if he promises to make something out of me, I'll follow him the rest of my life.* So he was captured by the promise of the Lord Jesus.

But he was also *captured* by the power of the Lord Jesus. Over in Luke 5 we have the experience of how Simon Peter was called to be a disciple of Jesus. It's a familiar passage. We are told here that Jesus borrowed Simon Peter's boat and used it for a pulpit. You remember that Jesus preached and taught the Word of God there, and then (verse 4) he turned to Simon and instructed, "Launch out into the deep; let down your net for a catch." Simon Peter was a fisherman by trade. Simon's business was catching fish. If there was anything Peter understood, it was how to catch fish. Jesus was a carpenter. Jesus was not a fisherman, and yet on this occasion Jesus had to establish his authority over the life of Peter and illustrate that he had power over sea as well as over land. Jesus Christ is not only landlord—he is sealord as well. Jesus Christ is in charge of the fish of the sea.

Simon said, "Master, we have toiled all night and have caught nothing, nevertheless at thy word, we will let down the nets." And the fish came from everywhere. Why, they were coming over the salty super slabs from lobster lane and from bass boulevard and from codfish corner. They were all trying to climb into the nets in obedience to the Lord Jesus. When Peter saw that, he made a marvelous discovery. He discovered that Jesus Christ has the power over his business life. There is something absolutely captivating about the power of Jesus Christ to control your business. Have you ever thought about selling out your business? You say, "Why, preacher, that's my livelihood. I wouldn't dare think of selling out. A few years ago a deacon friend of mine made a multimillion-dollar business out of frozen foods. One day he told me that he had decided to sell his business out. I looked at him like he was crazy, and asked him what he meant. He replied, "Well, I've decided to sell my business out to a subsidiary much bigger than mine, and I'm just going to manage the business for them. He made even more money than he had before when he sold out to a bigger business.

I'd like to suggest that all of you business people do that today. Why don't you sell out to a bigger business. I'm talking about the Lord Jesus Christ. Turn over your business to him. Why, Jesus sent fish Peter didn't know anything about, and he can send business you know nothing about as well, if you will surrender that business to the Lord Jesus and use what he gives you to his honor and glory. That got the attention of Simon Peter, and he fell on his knees before the feet of the Lord Jesus. Peter cried, "Depart from me. I am a sinful man, O Lord." Jesus said to him, "Fear not. From henceforth thou shalt catch men."

He was saying, "Simon, I'm going to take your business, and I'm going to expand your horizons, and I'm going to give your business eternal dimensions. You have been fishing for fish long enough, Simon Peter. I have the power to make you a fisher of men." If you will accept the concept that whatever you are doing in life can have eternal dimensions, and that wherever you are or whatever role you are filling in life can be used by Jesus to catch people alive for his glory, it will set your life on fire.

The Gospel of Mark states that after Jesus issued that call, the fisherman straight way left their nets and followed him. That was impulsive Peter. He didn't give it much thought. He didn't even check with his wife, didn't even go home, and say, "Listen, I'm going to follow Jesus." He straightway forsook his nets and followed the Lord. The Lord *captivated* the life of Simon Peter.

But there is a second thought. The Lord *constructed* his life.

Jesus said, "I'm going to make a rock out of you," but we know, of course, that rocks just don't happen. Rocks are the results of processing. It requires heat and pressure to produce a rock. You will discover that, though Peter was far from a rock in his character, the Lord Jesus skillfully shaped and molded his life. Jesus sent experiences into the life of Simon Peter to make a rock out of him.

I have selected three of those. The first one is in Matthew 14: 25-31. This experience is rather familiar to us. It is the experience of the disciples on the Sea of Galilee. Jesus was up there on the mountain praying. Then in verse 25 we are told that in the fourth watch of the night Jesus went unto them, walking on the sea. Now that must have been a sight to behold. Here was one of the great miracles of the Lord. Jesus had power over the realm of physical nature. Why, all Jesus had to do was speak the word, and he could turn the sea into jello under his feet, and simply go walking on the water. Simon Peter looked out there and saw the Lord coming. In verse 28, Peter said, "Lord if it be thou, bid me to come unto thee." Do you get the picture? Here was one of the greatest miracles that ever occurred. Impetuous Peter said, "Lord I want to get in on it, too." The Lord said, "Come on," and Peter jumped over the side of that boat, and walked on the water toward the Lord Jesus.

You say, "Wait a minute, I know the rest of the story. I know Peter made a fool of himself. I know he nearly drowned himself out there." True, but for a while he walked on the water! How far have you ever walked? How far have I ever walked? Most of us never leave the boat—except by accident. Most of us never trust God to do impossible things in our lives. In fact, I think what some of us ought to do is jump on out of the boat and trust ourselves totally to the Lord, and then see what Jesus can do in our lives. There was the experience of sinking. You had that experience in your life, Mr. Simon Peter. As you read you may have the experience of sinking.

There was a factor out there Simon hadn't thought about. He saw the wind "boisterous" (verse 30). He hadn't counted on the difficulties and problems of stepping out by faith and walking to the Lord Jesus Christ. That is consistent with his personality. He didn't think about the consequences. He just stepped out, and went toward the Lord—and he began to sink. The experience of sinking.

I'm writing, of course, about defeat. I'm talking about failure. Do you ever have that experience in your life? You know the Lord has called you to make something out of your life, and yet do you ever have a sinking experience? A defeat which leaves you humble is better than a victory which leaves you proud. It was good for Peter to sink. Can you imagine what it could have been if he had succeeded in walking on that water? Can you imagine if he had walked out there to Jesus and walked back to the boat? I can see him now, climbing into that boat with his chest all stuck out, buttons popping off his vest. I can see him easing up to the other fellows and saying, "Did you ever walk on water? Well, you're looking at one that did. It would have ruined him.

He had enough pride. He didn't need more pride. What he needed was humility, and here was the experience of sinking. Sometimes the Lord Jesus lets us fail to show us we are not what we ought to be, and that we need his help and power to become the rock he predicted we would be. Though Peter went down, he did not go under. And our Lord will never let you go under. He will always be there to rescue you, and to lift you up. The only thing Jesus said to him was a mild rebuke. "O thou of little faith, wherefore didst thou doubt?" I think Jesus was saying to Simon, "Simon, you are not a rock yet, you are just a little pebble."

Sometimes we think we're far down the pike to being what God wants us to be, and sometimes we become *proud* of our faith. Sometimes we think, *Lord, I've got it made. I'll never fall again. I'll never fail you again, Lord. Look at me: folks ought to be proud of what a great disciple I am.* Then, brother, our faith falters, our faith goes sinking down, and we discover how weak our faith really was. The experience of sinking.

Look at Matthew 16. Here is another experience in the life of Simon Peter, and this was a marvelous experience. In the gospel of Matthew you will discover that Jesus Christ was trying to teach his disciples two primary lessons. The first lesson was who he was. The second lesson was what he came to do. He had been teaching them who he was, and now came examination time. Jesus said (verse 13), "Whom do men say that I, the Son of man, am?" And they said, "Some say that you are John the Baptist, some say you are Elijah, others say you are Jeremiah, or one of the prophets. Then Jesus said, "But who do you day that I am?" Guess who answered? Simon Peter. He said, "Thou art the Christ, the Son of the living God. Jesus Christ said to Simon Peter, "Blessed art thou, Simon son of Jona, for flesh and blood hath not revealed it unto thee."

That was one of the highest hours in the life of Simon Peter. He climbed the heights in that experience. But now here is the experience I want you to see. First of all there was the experience of sinking, now there was the experience of swaying. In only a few seconds he swayed all the way from one place to another. Jesus began to teach about the cross. And when Jesus started talking about the cross, it disturbed Peter because he had big plans for Jesus. Verse 22 indicates "Peter took him." Peter probably laid his hands on Jesus, took him by the arm, there Peter was—grabbing God. He said, "Be it far from thee, Lord, this shall not be unto me." It was rather dangerous to rebuke God, wasn't it. Do you see how Peter swayed. One minute—"Thou art the Christ," the next minute— "No, don't go to the cross." Many of us want Jesus to make something out of our lives. We want to be that rock, but we don't want to go through the experience of the cross which is necessary for us to become what Jesus wants us to be.

Before the Simon in him could die, and before the rock could be constructed, he had to die to his old self, and he wasn't willing to do that. So, Jesus turned, looked at Simon Peter, and said unto him, "Get thee behind me, Satan." How do you suppose that made Simon Peter feel? "Lord, you are going to make a rock out of me, but on this occasion I'm acting more like Satan than a rock." Have you ever had that experience? You remark, "I'm just like Simon Peter." Keep listening—the experience of sinking, the experience of swaying.

Now look at Luke 22:31. Here is the third experience I want us to see. "And the Lord said Simon, Simon." Isn't it interesting that the Lord called him not by his new name but his old one? "Simon, Simon, Satan hath desired you to have you that he may sift you as wheat, but I have prayed for thee that thy faith fail thee not, and when thou art converted strengthen thy brethren." Jesus was saying to him, "Simon, you are still that old man. Simon, you are not yet a rock, and you are about to go through the experience of sifting. Satan wants to put you in his sieve and he is going to shake you now." You will notice the devil had to ask permission in order to get to Simon Peter.

If you are saved you are in the care of the Lord, and the only way the devil can touch your life is to obtain permission from the Lord. Do you remember Job and his experience? The devil had to gain permission to touch the life of Job and the same thing was true in the life of Simon Peter, yet Jesus realized there was some chaff in the life of Simon Peter and that it was necessary for the chaff to be sifted from his life. So, the Lord let Simon be buffeted by Satan, and the devil began to shake him and sift him. The result was that on three times Simon Peter denied his Lord. Now what did Satan put in Simon's way to cause him to deny the Lord Jesus?

There are three obstacles he put there. Number one, look at verse 33. After Jesus' statement Simon Peter said, "Lord, I am ready to go with thee, both into prison and to death." In one of the other gospels he said, "Though everybody else forsakes you, I won't, Lord. You can count on me." Do you know what his problem was? Presumption. That has happened to me so many times it's grievous to think about it. There have been those times when I have said, "Lord, you can count on me. Lord, I have given my life to you. Lord, I want to be 100 percent for you. Lord, I am going to go all the way with you. I'll die for you, Jesus." Hardly before I knew it I had done something which denied my Lord. Have you ever had that experience? Presumption.

The Bible declares, "Let him that thinketh he standeth, take heed lest he fall." Presumption.

The second thing is in verse 46—prayerlessness. Jesus asked, "Why sleep ye? rise and pray, lest ye enter into temptation." Simon Peter only a moment before had said, "Lord I'd die with you." Why, he wasn't prepared to die. He wasn't even prepared to pray. When we fail to pray and stay close to the Lord Jesus, if we are not very careful, we will deny him.

The third problem is in verse 54 and following. "And Peter followed afar off." In verse 55 he came to a fire and began to warm himself there. Then people started talking to him, and here was what they were saying. "Don't we recognize you? Aren't you one of the disciples of this man Jesus. Simon shook his head. "Nope. Not me." Haven't we seen you before? Aren't you one of those disciples. Peter replied, "Not I." Then a little girl came and said, "Yes, we know you. Your speech betrays you." Then Simon reverted to an old behavior pattern, something Simon Peter thought was far behind him in his Christian growth as God was making a rock out of him. He reverted to his old profanity. The Gospels state that with oaths and with cursing and with swearing Peter said, "I don't know the man."

About that time (in verse 61) "The Lord turned, and looked upon Peter." That word looked is the same word which is used in John 1, the first time Jesus ever saw Simon Peter. It was a look that penetrated him. Oh, it was not a look of condemnation. It was not a look of scorn. It was a look of love. Jesus looked into the life of Peter and he said, "Simon, the devil has sifted you, but don't forget, Simon, I'm praying for you." That look pulverized Peter, broke him to pieces, and "Peter went out, and wept bitterly" (v. 62).

If you are saved that doesn't mean necessarily that you won't sin. It doesn't mean that you cannot sin, but if you are saved you cannot sin and enjoy it. You just can't do it. I sin all I want to, but I also want to say I sin more than I want to. You see, I don't sin anymore, and when I do it breaks my heart, for I know that I am denying my Lord. I am then less than what he captured me to be. So underscore in your heart that the Lord captured him, underscore in your heart that the Lord constructed him, and then underscore in your heart that the Lord *converted* him. Did you notice that in verses 31 and 32? The Lord said to Simon, "I pray for you that your faith fail not, and when thou art converted. . . ." He is not talking about being saved. The word convert there means to return. And when you are returned, strengthen the brethren. The Lord was going to have to convert him. The Lord was going to have to turn him back.

We have the experience of the resurrection. Simon Peter ran to the empty tomb, saw that it was empty. A message was sent from the risen Lord, "Go tell my disciples *and Peter*." The Scriptures declare there was some private interview that Jesus had with Simon Peter. I think in those post-resurrection experiences that Simon Peter became totally convinced of the reality of the resurrection, but there was one thing of which he was not convinced—that his Lord could have any more use for him. And so Peter felt it was time to go back to the old life. In John 21, he was going back to the old ways. He had denied his Lord, he was ashamed, he was heartbroken. So in John 21:3, "Simon Peter saith unto them, I go a fishing." Being the leader he influenced the rest of them, and they said, "We also go with thee." He went back to the boats, back to the sea—and that night they fished and caught nothing.

Do you know what the Lord did? The Lord instructed all the fish to hide. The fish hid, and Simon Peter couldn't catch the first little minnow. The next morning, after a night of futility, after a night of operating on the basis of the old life, after a night of living like Simon, Peter saw that the Lord Jesus was on the shore. Jesus said, "Children, do you have any meat?" The Bible said they answered, and I think the loudest voice was that of Simon Peter as he called *no*! John recognized Jesus and he yelled, "It's the Lord." Simon Peter recognized that it was the Lord, put on his fisherman's coat, jumped into the water, and with strong strokes he came swimming to the shore.

In that breakfast experience the Lord *converted* Peter. How did he convert him? Two ways. Number one he converted him by recalling his failure. Have you noticed everything about this passage of Scripture recalls Simon Peter's failure? The Sea of Galilee was the same place he first met Jesus. Fishing. The same thing he was doing when he met the Lord. Bread. Simon Peter looked at that bread, and he must have remembered when Jesus took that bread and fed the five thousand. The Lord had asked, "Will you also go away? Simon Peter had answered, "Lord to whom shall we go? Thou hast the words of life."

He realized just like the rest, "I've left Him. Then what really pierced his heart was the fire of coals (v. 9). It reminded him of that same experience when he gathered around a fire of coals and denied that he ever knew the Lord. The Lord recalled his failures.

But then the Lord rekindled the fervor. After the meal was over Jesus looked over at Simon and he said (v.15), "Simon." Look at it—the same old name. "Simon, do you love me?" There is a little difference in the text that's not apparent in the English version. Jesus used the word *agape*, for love. Simon really said, "Lord, you know I like you." No more pride, no more presumption, no more impulsiveness. He had discovered that the Simon in him was a total failure. "Do you love me, Simon." "I like you."

The second time, "Simon, do you love me?" "Lord, you know I *like* you." And then the third time. Three times Jesus asked him that question. The third time, though, Jesus asked, "Simon, do you like me?" In other words, "Simon, I'm going to get right down there where you are, because I'm going to convert you." Simon was grieved and replied, "Lord, you know all things. "You know, you know, you know, I like you, and Jesus said, "all right, feed my sheep."

"I've got something for you to do, Simon. You have failed. You have gone through the experience of sinking and swaying and sifting. Now, Simon Peter, I want you to know I'm alive. I'll live in your heart forever. Go feed my sheep." Doesn't it thrill your heart when a few pages over in the Word you see this same man Simon Peter preaching on the day of Pentecost. He was a rock. Look at him. He was a rock, no longer wavering, no longer like the shifting sands. He was a rock, and with courage he preached the crucifixion of Jesus Christ, and he called men to repentance. Three thousand souls came to know Jesus.

And do you know what? From that point on everytime he is mentioned in the Scriptures he is referred to as Peter. When he is referred to as Simon in the book of Acts he is always spoken of as "Simon who is surnamed Peter." Do you see what Jesus did for him? Jesus called out of Simon the rock (Peter) that the Lord intended for him to be.

I have good news for you. This same Lord Jesus who made a rock out of this weak man calls to you. He says, "Come follow me, and I will make everything out of you that you ought to be." Would you like to be a rock? Would you like Jesus to take the you that you are and transform you into the you that you ought to be?

3.
The Traitor

John 13:18-30

Many names will go down in infamy. Hitler, Stalin, Ivan the Terrible, Mao tse tung, Idi Amin. But the most despicable name in all of human history is the name of Judas.

The name Judas itself was a very noble name for it meant "praise." Judas Iscariot took that noble name and brought it down to death. On the other hand, the Lord Jesus took a rather ordinary, common name and exalted it to the heights as he lifted it by his life.

But the name of Judas is a name of infamy. It is a name that we avoid. We wouldn't even name our dogs Judas, much less name our children after the man who is known in the Bible as the one who betrayed the Son of God. Whenever we think about Judas we shudder, for he lived perhaps the lowest life in the pages of human history.

In Dante's Inferno he pictures us going down to the lowest part of the pit where the worst of all sinners are. In the midst of the pit is the devil himself, and in the teeth of the devil is Judas Iscariot being torn to pieces. Dante in this view of hell was trying to convey his view that the most despised, most despicable, darkest sinner who ever lived was Judas Iscariot. In recent days there seems to have been an effort to reclaim the life of Judas and make him somewhat of a hero. A few years ago a rock musical, "Jesus Christ Superstar," presented Judas as rather a hero and a hopeless victim of the circumstances. In recent days movies have portrayed Judas Iscariot as a rather good kind of guy. He is not so painted by the brush of the Scriptures.

31

The Lord Jesus Christ said that it would have been good for that man if he had never been born. In the Bible Judas is given many titles. He is referred to as the betrayer, a devil, a thief, and "the son of perdition." But I believe the name Luke gives him in 6:16 of his Gospel is the title that sears our ears when we hear it. Luke calls him the "traitor," Judas the traitor who betrayed our Lord.

There have been many traitors in history. We remember Benedict Arnold as the man who betrayed his country. I am told that somewhere in New York state there is a monument which was built to Revolutionary War heroes. There are four places around that monument, and there are three statues to various generals in the Revolutionary War. The fourth space is vacant, for it was intended to be the space for Benedict Arnold, but Benedict Arnold became a traitor. Benedict Arnold will go down in history as an infamous traitor but not like Judas, for Judas was a traitor of the Son of God, the Lord of glory himself.

Caesar was pictured as being betrayed by Brutus, and Shakespeare wrote that when Caesar was stabbed in the heart by his own friend, Brutus, he cried, "You, too, Brutus? This was the unkindest cut of all."

I think that gives us an inkling of how the Son of God must have felt as he was betrayed by one of his own, one of the twelve apostles—Judas Iscariot himself. Consider the inmost thoughts of the Son of God concerning the betrayal of Judas, as it is given to us in prophecy. In Psalms 55:12 and following, we have the thoughts of our Lord reflected. "For it was not an enemy that reproached me; then I could have borne it: neither was it he that hated me that did magnify himself against me; then I would have hid myself from him: But it was thou, a man mine equal, my guide and mine acquaintance. We took sweet counsel together, and walked unto the house of God in company." Then in verse 21 it says the words of his mouth were smoother than butter, but war was in heart: his words were softer than oil, yet they were drawn swords."

How terrible it must have been when the Lord Jesus looked at one of his own, the traitor who betrayed him. Judas was one of the twelve, and he is one of the darkest riddles in all of the Bible. It's hard to understand how Judas would have been chosen to be a disciple of the Lord Jesus, and yet we know that he was placed in a position of unusual honor and privilege. Judas had the opportunity to see Jesus perform many miracles. Judas heard the prayers of Jesus as he touched heaven, but none of these things seemed to have helped Iscariot. All of these were like pouring water on a dead stick which will never grow and will sooner or later will rot.

He was the traitor, betraying the Son of God for thirty pieces of silver. You say, "Well, preacher I'll never do that! I don't care what I may do. I'll never betray the Son of God." I'm going to stun you —some who read this could betray him.

First, I want you to notice the *priority* of his life. Judas was a man who had a priority, that which was absolutely first in his life. It was this priority that became the cancer eating away at the soul of Judas Iscariot. This passage states that Judas had "the bag" (v. 29). Judas was the treasurer of our Lord's disciples. The money placed in the treasury of the disciples was in the disposal and care of Judas. You see, it may be that this revealed something about the priority of his life as well. Judas was a man in love with material possessions, and he had made his love his profession. He was obsessed with it.

It's a rather unusual story which tells us how this priority is revealed. In John 12 I want you to see that story. It is the moving story of Mary anointing the feet of Jesus Christ with a box of expensive perfume. She poured that perfume lavishly upon the feet of the Son of God, and the house was filled with the odor of the ointment. It was in this setting of generosity, it was in this response to this act of lavishness upon the Lord that Judas revealed the priority of his life, so I want you to notice the response of Judas Iscariot in verses 4 and 5. "Then saith one of his disciples, Judas Iscariot which should betray him, why was not this ointment sold for three hundred pence and given to the poor?"

You see this was the experience which trapped Judas Iscariot. It revealed the priority of his life.

They tell me that sometimes over in Africa the natives have a rather ingenious method of catching monkeys. They take a coconut shell, cut a hole in it just large enough for a monkey's hand to go through, and then they fill that coconut shell with fruit. When the monkey reaches in the shell and gets a handful of the fruit, they have the monkey because he's so greedy he won't release the fruit to let his hand escape.

This experience was the trap which caught Judas and revealed the priority, the preeminent love of his life. Judas loved material things. Verse 6 declares that Judas said what he did, not because he cared for the poor, but because he was a thief. No doubt Judas had been stealing from the treasury all along. Judas had been feathering his own nest from the treasury from time to time. So, when Judas was confronted by a person who was generous in their love for the Lord Jesus, it is more than Judas was able to bear. Isn't it rather interesting that the generosity of one person toward the Lord evoked criticism from the life of Judas Iscariot. I have always noticed this tendency on the part of Judas's personality.

A few years ago in Atlanta, Georgia, two projects were going on almost side by side. One was a project to build a marvelous house of worship where the Lord Jesus Christ would be preached. The other was a stadium where games would be played. The church building was a mammoth project. It was going to cost two million dollars. The stadium, on the other hand, was going to cost twenty million dollars, and yet I heard a great deal of criticism toward the church. I heard people saying, "That's too much money to spend on building a church. That's wasting money. You ought not to spend that much money on a church, but never one time did I hear a single critical word about spending twenty million dollars to build a stadium. Isn't it strange how the generosity of one toward the Lord evokes criticism from a Judas personality.

My friend, how you respond to what people do for the Lord Jesus speaks volumes about you. In fact, in one of the other Gospels we are told that Judas regarded what the woman had done as a waste. But nothing is ever wasted if it is bestowed on the Lord Jesus Christ. So here was Judas. He was a thief, he didn't really care for the poor, and the chant here, "take care of the poor," is the same chant often led by the hypocrites of the church in our day. Those who would bestow the most love on the Lord Jesus Christ are those who are actually the most concerned about the social concerns of the world around us. It is never right to neglect the things of the

Lord to carry out an altruistic purpose that you have in your own mind, no matter how good the purpose.

Now I want you to see how the Lord rebuked him, for we are told in verse 7 that Jesus asked, "Let her alone against the day of my burial hath she kept this, for the poor always you have with you, but me . . ." Jesus was saying, "Judas, this ought to be the priority of your life, *me*. I must be first in your life." Now Jesus had given warnings to Judas all along. Judas had heard Jesus teach, "Beware of covetousness." Judas had heard our Lord when he asked, "What shall it profit a man, if he gain the whole world and lose his own soul?" And yet there was a priority that mastered the life of Judas, material things. This should be a tremendous warning to our heart.

You see, Judas was often *at* the side of Jesus, but he was never *on* the side of Jesus. He saw the miracles. He was closely associated with the Son of God, and yet he never really *knew* him in a personal kind of relationship. You take a bottle and seal it, then place it in the ocean, and it will remain dry in the midst of the water. You take a heart and seal it to the love of Jesus Christ, and it will remain sealed against the things of God amid the holiest associations. Is there a Judas reading this? Is there a Judas here today? You say, "Oh, not me!" Wait a minute. Don't you turn me off. Don't you say, "It can't be me." Is there a priority in your life that may cause you one of these days to betray the Son of God?

There is a second idea I want us to see from this study of Judas, now let's consider the *propensity* of life. Propensity means an inclination toward something. It means a tendency, a leaning in a certain direction. As you study the life of Judas Iscariot, you will discover that there was a propensity toward betrayal, a tendency in his life to betray. Now it's always like that. When a person makes the material his priority, his propensity is toward betrayal of Jesus Christ.

Let's go back to the passage at the beginning, and I want to show you how this propensity is revealed. First of all, it is revealed in John 13:18, for there Jesus said, "I speak not of you all. I know whom I have chosen (watch him) but that the scripture may be fulfilled." Then he quoted Psalm 41:9: "He that eateth bread with me hath lifted up his heel against me." That, my friends, is one of the most incisive verses on the life of Judas Iscariot in all of the Bible, "he that eateth bread with me hath lifted up his heel." Literally the wording there is, "he hath made great his heel." It is a picture of violent hatred, of utter contempt. It is a picture of the propensity toward betrayal.

If Judas had ever read his Bible, he would have discovered his own picture in the pages of the Book. That is why some people never open the Bible, because they see themselves in its pages. I heard about an Oriental monarch who bought a Bible and hired an interpreter to come and read it to him. As the interpreter read the Bible, the monarch cried out, "The men who made that book made me!" And that is right. As you open up your Bible you will see the propensity of your life, you will see the picture of the human heart as it is in all of its darkness and in all of its depravity. The Scriptures reveal the propensity toward betrayal in his life.

But not only did the Scriptures do it, but the Savior himself did it. Look at what Jesus said in verse 21. He was troubled in spirit, and then Jesus specifically said to his disciples gathered around that Passover meal. "Verily, verily, I say unto you, that one of you shall betray me." Jesus had been predicting betrayal all along. You remember back in John 6:64 Jesus knew from the beginning who would betray him. I find that a mystery. From the very beginning Jesus knew who would betray him, and then down in verse 70 Jesus said "Have I not chosen twelve of you, and one of you is a devil?" Then, having predicted betrayal all along, then came the night before the cross, and Jesus asserted, "One of you shall betray me." That statement from their Lord shook them to their bootstraps. It tore them up.

In fact, if you will read the parallel account that Matthew gives, you will discover that when Jesus spoke those words, they were all exceedingly sorrowful and everyone of them began to ask, "Lord, is it I? Lord, is it I?" Everyone of them. When Jesus said, "One of you shall betray me," it was like a scapel that cut to the very depths of their beings. Looking into the inner recesses of their hearts those disciples made a startling discovery. They discovered that the potential for betrayal was in all of their hearts. The potential to betray the Lord Jesus Christ is in the heart of every person. Most of us have already, at one time or another, betrayed the Son of God. They saw the potential in their hearts, and so Jesus revealed it.

Jesus had done everything in his power to provoke the conscience of Judas and to stop him from the course to which he had committed himself. Jesus had tried to warn him up until the last. Now let's watch Judas's behavior. We are told that they all began to wonder who it was. You see, no one suspected Judas. Nobody would have dreamed it was Judas Iscariot. Judas Iscariot had the life of an outward saint but the heart of the devil. When those disciples looked around, he was the last one they would have picked. Why, Judas was a member of the twelve. He was a part of the group. He was actively involved in the activities of the Lord Jesus Christ, but Christ, who knows the hearts of people, looked into his heart and said, "You will betray me." There are thousands of people in this world who are hiding behind baptismal certificates. There are thousands who are hiding behind their receipts of contributions to the churches. There are thousands who are sitting on "boards" of deacons, who are teaching Sunday School classes, who are singing in church choirs, and yet in their hearts the Lord Jesus Christ would speak to them, "You will betray me before it's over."

Back in the second verse of this thirteenth chapter we are told that the devil had already put it into Judas's heart to betray Jesus. The devil looked around for someone whose heart was black enough to receive the satanic suggestion of betrayal, and he found the heart of Judas Iscariot. And then, of all things, Judas said, "Lord, is it I?" That very moment the blood money was safely tucked away under his robes. "Lord, is it I?"

If you had told Judas three years prior that he would betray the Son of God, he would have laughed you to scorn. We rarely ever think we will do what we eventually do. If I were to tell you that five years from now, you might be an addict, or that five years from now you will be a thief, or that five years from now you will be a drunkard, or that five years from now you will sell out the Lord Jesus Christ for less than thirty pieces of silver, you would laugh me to scorn. "Preacher, it will never ever be." Oh, you hadn't looked at it that way? Is there a young lady who has been thinking of yielding her purity to an insistent boyfriend. If so, she will sell out the One who shed his blood that she might be pure. Is there a businessman considering entering into a questionable business deal? If he does, he is betraying the One who died that he might be honest. A preacher friend of mine received a letter two weeks ago from one of the young men in his congregation. In this letter the man simply wrote to his pastor, "Pastor, pastor, I quit. I'm through with the Christian life. It's too hard. It's too difficult. It's too demanding. I've tried it, and it just doesn't work, and I have made up my mind to throw it all overboard. I have made up my mind—I'm going to do it my way. I'm going to do my thing. I'm going to please myself. I'm going to live it up. I'm going to have a big time. I'm through with the church." He signed the letter "yours truly" with his name, and under his name he wrote, Judas Iscariot. He was probably more honest than others.

Now the Lord did everything he could to stop Judas. I have an idea that Judas was placed in the position of honor that night. I believe that the head of the Lord Jesus Christ leaned on the chest of Judas that night. Everything done that night was designed by the Lord to prick the conscience of Judas Iscariot. Can you imagine how the head of Jesus Christ must have burned a hole to the heart of Judas Iscariot? When Jesus got on his hands and knees and washed the feet of his own betrayer, don't you know the water scalded the feet of Judas Iscariot? Then the Lord extended the highest expression of friendship and affection when he handed Judas the sop.

Where I came from in the country I used to hear them talk about sopping gravy. I didn't know what in the world a sop was. A sop is merely a piece of bread dipped in juices. It's a morsel of food, and the Lord extended that morsel as if to say, "Oh, friend of mine, I have placed you tonight in the highest position of honor. Don't you think that broke the heart, the hard crust of Judas. No, it didn't. It didn't. For the Scriptures declare in verse 27, "After the sop . . . satan. Listen friends, it's a very short step from satanic *suggestion* to satanic *possession*.

I can imagine that the voice of Judas's conscience was whisper-

ing, to him, "Give it up, Judas. Confess, fall at his feet, Judas.
Don't do it, Judas, you are a fool, Judas. Don't do it!" But it was
too late. His hand was already on the door, he opened that door,
and the Bible says "he went immediately out, and it was night."
It's always night when you go away from the Lord Jesus. As I study
the life of Judas I see the priority in his life and the propensity of
his life.

There is then the profanity of his life. "Oh," you ask,
"Preacher, did he use bad language?" No, I use the word profanity
in its truest sense. A profane person is one who has no room whatsoever in his life for God. A profane man is one who has utter contempt and disregard for God. Every line of Judas's story becomes
blacker and blacker, for Judas is a picture of the darkness and
depths to which the human heart will go. I see his profanity in his
agreement with betrayal.

He went to the chief priest and the scribes. They had been looking for an opportunity to arrest the Lord Jesus Christ, and here was
one of his own ready to deliver the Son of God to them. They were
delighted. Why, this exceeded their fondest expectations that one
of his own would betray him. I wonder if the powers of darkness
are singing in glee because some of you have offered to sell out the
Lord. Judas bargained, "What will you give me for him?" Can
you imagine that? He was selling the Lord Jesus Christ at the price
of the buyer, and they offered to give him the price of a common
slave, thirty pieces of silver. He took those thirty pieces of silver
and bound them to him, and it wasn't many hours until the heinous
act of betrayal. Judas had gone to make the arrangements to deliver Him.

Jesus had gone to the garden of Gethsemane, and there Jesus
Christ was bowed in prayer. He was praying like no man on this
earth has ever prayed, and he had made the final surrender to the
death of the cross. He prayed, "Father, not my will, but thine be
done." The Scriptures relate that the drops of his sweat became great
drops of blood. That is why the soldiers were alarmed. That is why
they were so shaken when they saw the Lord Jesus. When Jesus
came out of that garden of Gethsamene and the soldiers met him,
his hair, his beard, and his face were soaked with blood. They gave

Judas a band of soldiers. It could have been two hundred to six hundred soldiers. If we use the smaller figure, can you imagine two hundred soldiers coming to arrest an unarmed Galilean carpenter?

As Jesus walked out of that garden, the crowd approached. They saw the flashing of the torches in the night, the glitter of the lanterns in the night. They heard the clashing of the swords, and then the Son of God looked at the mob. John 18:5 states, "Judas stood with them." Listen, a person will always stand where his heart is. Where do you stand? When an issue is at stake, where do you stand? When the cause of Jesus Christ is under attack, where do you stand. When a matter of morals and decency is up for grabs, where do you stand? May God help us never to be standing *against* him, but always standing *with* him.

But I not only see where he stood—I hear what he said. He had a prearranged signal. Judas said, "I want you to be sure and get the right man." So he stepped out from the crowd, came to the Lord Jesus, and said, "Hail, Master." And the Bible says he kissed him. I can hear the hiss in that kiss. That kiss was filled with the venom of hell. Here was a man who kissed the gate of heaven and went to hell. When he withdrew his lips from the Son of God, the blood of Jesus may have trickled down Judas's face, the very blood that would be shed for him on a gory cross. Jesus said, "Friend, friend, wherefore art thou come. Friend, betrayest thou the Son of God with a kiss?" as if Jesus were reaching out one more time in mercy. "Friend, think what you are doing"—friend, and it was the last recorded word Jesus ever spoke to Judas.

But that was not the end of the story. That was not the end of the picture. The Word says that when they condemned Jesus, Judas realized what he had done, and Matthew tells us that it "repented him." His conscience began to bother him, to torment him. Those pieces of silver began to burn holes in his hand. He couldn't live with his conscience. I heard about a man who was acquitted of murder, who later on wrote his lawyer: "You saved me from the electric chair, but not from my conscience." Did Jesus repent. Not on your life! It's a different word altogether. The Greek word which indicates Gospel repentance unto salvation was a word which meant a godly sorrow which leads to repentance. But it's a different word here. It is not the word for genuine repentance. It was a word which meant remorse and regret. He was filled with remorse and regret, and so he ran into the Temple. He said to the chief priest, "Here, take your money. I don't want your money." And they said, "You just do what you want to do with it." So Judas took those thirty pieces of silver and flung them to the pavement below, and every piece rang, "Traitor, traitor, traitor."

And Judas went out to the field of blood, and in that field of blood, he took a rope, threw it across a limb of a tree, made a noose, tightened it around his neck, and he swung himself out into eternity. The flames of hell already were leaping around him and each flame was sizzling, "Traitor, traitor, traitor." His body fell headlong and burst asunder, and his bowels gushed out. The rope swinging in the wind hissing, "Traitor, traitor, traitor, traitor . . . and "he went to his own place." Where was that, preacher? He went to hell. He went to heaven's graveyard. He want to eternity's penitentiary. He went to creation's insane asylum. He went to hell. Why? He was a traitor. He was a Judas.

I have often wondered what would have happened if, instead of going toward the field of blood, Judas had turned and gone toward Jesus and had fallen before his feet, and cried, "Oh, Lord Jesus, I sold you out! Oh, Lord Jesus, I put material things first. Oh, Lord Jesus, I had a propensity toward betrayal, Oh, Jesus, I have been a profane man. I have had no room for God in my life, but, Lord Jesus, I see the error of my ways. I repent. I ask your forgiveness. Come into my life and change me." What do you think about it? I fully believe that the Lord Jesus Christ would have reached out his arms of mercy, forgiveness, and love, and brought Judas into the very family of God. But Judas didn't do it, and it is too late for Judas today. Judas sits upon a throne of fire in hell today, and the epitaph over his throne in hell reads, "Judas Iscariot, the traitor."

Too late, but it is not too late for you. It's not too late for you. There is time for you. You can repent. You can come to Jesus. You can quit hiding behind your religiosity and your church membership. You can come to Jesus Christ and let him save you.

4.
The Late Mr. Thomas

John 20:24-29

When Jesus Christ was raised from the dead, the Bible declares that "he showed himself alive" in a series of post-resurrection appearances. In Acts 1:3 we are told that Jesus proved himself to be alive to his disciples by "many infallible proofs." These appearances of the Lord Jesus have come to be tremendous evidences for the reality of the resurrection.

There are occasions after his resurrection when Jesus revealed himself to large numbers of people. On one occasion he revealed himself to over 500 at one time. At other times he made himself known to The Twelve, but there were also instances where Jesus revealed himself for the particular benefit of one individual. He revealed himself to Simon Peter and restored him. He revealed himself to Mary Magdalene and rekindled her love. He revealed himself to James, his half brother, and generated faith in his heart.

I believe that this particular appearance to Thomas was for the purpose of restoring Thomas and stirring faith and conviction in his heart. Thomas, as you know, was one of the twelve apostles of the Lord Jesus, and I am constantly amazed by the different personalities we find in the men who followed the Lord Jesus Christ. There was Simon Peter, the rugged, the rough, the outspoken one who was constantly opening his mouth. By way of contrast here is Thomas. Thomas seems rarely to have spoken, and when Thomas did speak he seems to have been rather gloomy, rather despondent of personality.

There are two other times in the Gospel of John where Thomas spoke. The first time is in John 11 where Jesus talked about going to raise Lazarus from the dead, and Thomas was so sure Jesus was going to meet his death on that occasion that he suggested to the rest of the disciples "Let us go with him that we may die with him." The second time Thomas spoke was in that marvelous fourteenth chapter of John where Jesus had promised the disciples, "Where I go you know, and the way you know." But Thomas was not going to admit something that he didn't believe, and he was not going to say something was so when he didn't feel that it was. Thomas responded to the Lord with, "Lord, we don't know where you're going, and how can we know the way?" Jesus replied, "I am the way, the truth, and the life. No man cometh unto the Father but by me."

Thomas seemed to have been a doubter. When all of the other people were rejoicing in the resurrection of the Lord Jesus, Thomas was wandering around in the wilderness of doubt. I do believe that Thomas was an honest doubter. Someone said that doubt is the agony of an earnest soul, or it is the trifling of some superficial fool. I am convinced that the former was true of Thomas. I believe Thomas made the mistake of doubting his beliefs and believing his doubts, and so the Lord Jesus Christ manifested himself to him, and Thomas was cured from his doubt.

When you read this passage carefully, you see Thomas in two different scenes. First of all, we see Thomas missing the risen Christ, and then we see Thomas meeting the risen Christ. First of all, in verses 24 and 25, let's consider together Thomas missing the risen Christ. When Jesus revealed himself to the other disciples, Thomas was not there. He missed the risen Lord. I have an idea that there are multitudes of people who will have the sad experience that Thomas had on that occasion. Thousands of people will enter beautiful buildings, they will hear the choirs singing about the resurrection of the Lord, they will be donned in beautiful Easter clothing, and they will hear sermons about the resurrection of the Lord Jesus Christ. Yet, they will miss the risen Christ, and they will never know him in a personal experience. Thomas knew the facts about the resurrection of Jesus, but they were not real to him because he had missed the risen Christ.

There is a great deal of discussion about why Thomas was absent on that particular Lord's evening. There are some who claim that Thomas had lost his love for the Lord Jesus, but I don't believe that for a moment. I do not believe that Thomas was absent because he had lost his love for the Lord Jesus, but I feel that Thomas was not there out of sheer despondency of spirit. He seems to have been rather pessimistic in his disposition. He seems always to have looked on the dark, gloomy side of things. The events of the crucifixion and the horror of Jesus' dying on the cross of Calvary were so dreadful and so devastating to the personality of Thomas that, in utter heartbreak, he sought a place of aloneness and separation.

Thomas did the very worst thing you can do if you are a despondent person by nature. A bad course of action when you are going through a despondent period is to withdraw yourself from the fellowship of those who love you, pull yourself into a shell, and merely muddle around in the waters of doubt. So he missed the risen Christ. When he did it led him to three things. First of all, missing the risen Christ led Thomas to an unhealthy pessimism. The disciples were all excited, and they were all happy. They came announcing to Thomas, "We have seen the Christ. We have seen the Lord!" But Thomas wouldn't have any of that. Thomas at that time was a pessimistic Thomas. He could not accept that it was so. Here was the testimony of ten of his closest friends. Here was the testimony of competent witnesses, and yet Mr. Thomas was a pessimist. Somebody remarked that a pessimist is a person who feels bad when he feels good, for fear that he is going to feel worse when he feels better. Well, I think that is the kind of person Thomas was. I heard about two pessimists who met one another at a party, and instead of shaking hands they shook heads. That was Thomas's situation. He shook his head in despondency and pessimism.

Now Thomas was a pessimist because he had missed the service. If you will notice back in verse 19, when Jesus revealed himself to the other disciples, it was on the first day of the week, the Lord's Day. It was in the evening service, but Brother Thomas was not there. I want to remind you of the fact that you lose out when you miss the services at the house of God. Every Lord's Day we gather together, and we celebrate the resurrection of Jesus Christ. The very day on which we worship is a testimony to the resurrection. The "eighth," day is the day of completeness. The eighth day is that first day of the week when Jesus Christ was raised from the dead. When you absent yourself from the services of God you are inviting a pessimism into your life by failing to be present in the services.

The disciples of the Lord Jesus had the same problem that we often face. We are in the services, God is blessing, and the power of God comes down, and it is glorious to behold. Then we try to explain that service to a person who was not there, and we discover that it is difficult to communicate how God blessed a service to someone who was not there. In Hebrews 10:25 we are warned of the danger of missing the house of God and the services. We are not to forsake the assembling of ourselves together. Thomas was a pessimist because he missed the service.

I think all of us can identify with the pessimism of Thomas. I find myself in a rather pessimistic vein so many times. I suppose that all of us have been "had" so many times that we tend to be pessimistic. I find myself watching commercials, and I'm very much of a pessimist. I ask myself, "I wonder if it will really pick up as much dust as it says it will. I wonder if that food is actually as good as they claim it is. I wonder if that program is truly going to accomplish what they say it will." There is a tendency for us to move in the direction of pessimism, to want to be unbelieving and to want to doubt. When you miss the risen Christ it leads you to an unhealthy pessimism.

Secondly, it led him, not only to an unhealthy pessimism, but to an *unholy dogmatism*. Look how dogmatic Thomas became in verse 25. They said, "We have seen the Lord," but Thomas said, "Except I shall see in his hands the print of the nails, and put my finger into the print of the nails, and thrust my hand into his side, I will not believe." He was awfully dogmatic. He was presuming to prescribe to the God of this universe how He must reveal himself. There are many people who want to dictate conditions to God and instruct God how he must do things. They try to tell the God who created us and the God who let his Son die on the cross how he must come into our hearts. Mr. Thomas adopted the philosophy that "seeing is believing." In fact, if you will notice, that is exactly what he said. He said, "Unless I see I will not believe. " Many people assume that position today.

Now the tragedy is we don't operate on that basis in daily life. We don't operate on a seeing-is-believing basis, but rather we operate on the basis of faith in so many of the matters of daily life. For instance, it's time for you to go to work in the morning, and there is your car. Well, you don't operate on a seeing-is-believing basis. You don't say, "Unless I can see the factory where that car was built, and unless I can see the workmen who worked on that car, I'm not going." You just climb into it by faith. You accept that it has been put together properly and you go to work. You sit down to eat your noon meal. You don't operate on the basis of seeing is believing. You operate on the basis of faith. You don't look at that food, and say unless I can see the plant where that food has been processed, and unless I can see the man that planted the seed in the ground, I am not going to believe in the reality and in the nutrition of that food. Isn't it a rather apparent fact that we operate on the basis of faith in matters of daily life, and yet when it comes to matters of eternal life we want to reverse the process and protest, "Except I can see I will not believe. Jesus was very specific in the matter, and he said in verse 29, "Thomas, blessed are those who have not seen and yet believe." But Thomas had an unholy dogmatism. He was in a frame of mind that was trying to tell the Lord exactly how God was going to have to do it.

I could spend a considerable time giving you a rational reason to accept the reality of the resurrection. The resurrection of Jesus Christ is the best-documented fact in the history of the world. The records are impeccable. There is absolutely no basis intellectually to question the reliability of the documentation that Jesus Christ rose from the dead. There is more documentation of the resurrection than there is of many facts in American history. There is more proof that Jesus Christ rose from the dead than there is of the existence of the Spanish-American War or the Civil War. There is every adequate reason to believe in the resurrection of Jesus Christ. But you don't primarily come to Jesus that way. You don't come to the Lord Jesus through the reason gate, but rather through the faith gate.

Romans 10:9 asserts: "If thou shalt confess with thy mouth the Lord Jesus, and believe in thine heart [not head] that God hath raised him from the dead, thou shalt be saved." Here was his unholy dogmatism. He was pretending to tell the Lord how to deal with his life.

Not only did missing the risen Christ lead him to an unholy dogmatism, it also moved him to an unhappy skepticism. He said emphatically in verse 25, "I will not believe." In the Greek language it was a double negative. Now in the Greek language that was good grammar, but in the English language that was bad grammar. We don't say, "I'll not not do something." We consider that poor grammar. In Greek they used a double negative for emphasis, and literally he was saying here, "Except I see I will not not believe." Here he had an unhappy skepticism. He was a skeptic. I will not believe!

This is a day of skepticism. There are all kinds of skeptics around us. There is the scientific skeptic who declares that unless God will come down into the narrow dimensions of his test tube and let him analyze God, he will not not believe. There is the philosophical skeptic who feels that unless God will confine himself to rational dimensions he will not believe. There is the religious skeptic who says that unless God will restrict himself to his narrow definitions of religion, he will not believe.

That is an untenable position. It is totally impossible for you to say, "I do not believe." Every person believes something. You say, "Well, preacher, you have missed it today. I'm an agnostic. I don't believe in anything." "I'm an atheist. I don't believe there is anything to the resurrection of the Lord Jesus. I don't believe anything." Let me ask you a question or two. You don't believe there is anything? Right? I don't believe that. Do you believe your belief is correct. *Do you believe that you don't believe.* So you believe in your unbelief, and thus you do believe something! Yours is an obsolutely untenable position, and you will notice that Thomas betrayed himself when he said, "I will not believe." He didn't say, "I *cannot* believe." That is not the problem. The problem is not that you cannot exercise your faith intellectually. In fact, Jesus said on one occasion if you had faith the size of a grain of mustard seed you could remove mountains. I was over in the Holy Land and we were visiting the site of King David's ancient palace. As we came to the entrance our guide walked over to a bush and grabbed some little-bitty things. He showed them to me and asked, "Do you know what that is." I said no. They were grains of mustard seed. They were so small, and yet Jesus taught that if you had just a little grain of faith, just the size of a grain of mustard seed, you could move mountains.

Listen, the Scriptures say that God has given to every man "a measure of faith." Every person has the ability to believe in the Lord Jesus Christ. When God created a human being, God gave that human being the capacity of conviction. God created that person with the faculty of faith, and it is not the problem that you cannot believe. The problem is: you will not believe. The problem is not in the intellect. The problem is in the will. Jesus remarked on one occasion, "You will not come to me that you might have life." He did not say, "You cannot come to me."

So here was Mr. Thomas. He was in a state of unhappy skepticism, and he was the loser for it. You are always the loser when you chose to adopt the position of skepticism. You are always the loser when you refuse to come to God in God's way. Imagine you have in your hand a transistor radio, and you are in unhappy pessimism and skepticism. You turn on that transistor radio, and they are playing "Because he lives," and you flick it off. You will have none of that. And you say, "There, I've eliminated that foolish music. It is gone." No, you didn't do away with the music. You didn't eliminate the music. All you did was cut off your reception of that music, and you see, Jesus Christ is alive whether anybody in the world believes it or not. Jesus Christ is alive, and if you chose by an act of your will not to believe it, you have not eliminated the reality of the resurrection. You have not done away with the fact that Jesus Christ is alive in this world today. All you have done is cut off your reception of it, and you will confine yourself to the despondency of unhappy skepticism. Thomas missed the risen Christ.

I want you to see the second thought. Not only did we view him *missing* the risen Christ, but we see Thomas *meeting* the risen Christ. It must have been a rough week for Thomas. Eight days in despondency, in despair and in doubt. Eight days later, the Bible says, Thomas was with them—then came Jesus. Isn't that just like the Lord? Isn't it wonderful to know that the Lord comes to us again and again? And on this occasion when Mr. Thomas met the risen Christ, there were three results from that meeting. There was, first of all, demonstration. Oh, I love to behold the marvelous condescension of the Lord Jesus Christ on this occasion, for Thomas had said, "Except I see those nail prints in his hands, I am not going to believe," and it's as if the Lord Jesus condescends to the level of the weak faith of Thomas. In essence Jesus was saying, "All right, Thomas, if that is as high as you can reach, I will come down there to the level of your faith. Thomas, I want to show you the wounds in my hands. Thomas, I want to show you the scar in my side. Thomas, be not faithless but believing. Shake off this despair. Shake off this doubt, and allow yourself to move from the dungeon of doubt into the tabernacle of trust." So Jesus Christ showed him his hands and his side, and Thomas saw the wounds of the Lord Jesus. When Thomas saw those wounds it was a reminder to him of what Jesus had done on the cross for him.

Easter is the day when we celebrate the resurrection of the Lord Jesus. It is the day when we rejoice together that Jesus Christ is no longer in the tomb, that Christ is no longer impaled upon a Roman cross—that he is alive. But we should never allow ourselves to forget that two thousand years ago Jesus Christ was indeed crucified on the cross, that those hands of the Son of God were indeed driven by nails to that wooden cross, that there was indeed a spear that was cast into the side of the Son of God, and that blood and water did indeed flow from his side, and that by those wounds we are healed. There is salvation in the crucifixion of the Lord Jesus, and don't ever forget his wounds.

I heard about a man who had fought in the Civil War and had developed a real hostility and hatred toward his general, General Gordon. After the war (they were both from South Carolina), General Gordon was scheduled to be elected the governor of the state. The legislature was going to vote on the matter, and this officer once under General Gordon had decided that he would embarrass the general by casting his vote against him in the legislature. The day of the election came, and the men began to cast their ballots in the legislature. As they came closer and closer to this man, he was planning to embarrass General Gordon. But when it came time for him to vote he looked at the General, saw the scars and the wounds which the General had received in battle, and the man broke down and began to weep. He wailed, "I can't do it. I can't do it. I had forgotten the scars. I had forgotten the scars." Don't ever forget the scars, don't ever forget those wounded hands of the Lord Jesus.

Thomas saw the wounds. He heard the words. Jesus repeated almost identically the words Thomas himself had said. I can imagine how embarrassed Thomas was when he heard his own words on the lips of the Savior. Can you imagine how ashamed Thomas was when he heard the living Son of God enunciating Thomas's own doubt, skepticism, dogmatism, paganism, and pessimism. When Thomas heard those words they sounded so inadequate, so carnal, so faithless on the lips of the Son of God, and Thomas had a demonstration of the reality of the Lord Jesus.

I am convinced in my heart if you are honest, sincere, and really want to know the Lord Jesus Christ as your Savior, the Lord will make himself known to you, and will become real in a saving way. A few years ago I was pastor of a church near Chattanooga, Tennessee, and I was visiting in the home of an unsaved man, and one of the verses I pressed on his heart was Romans 10:9. I couldn't draw him right on into the kingdom of God, and so I left him with that verse. I reminded him, "I'll tell you what you do. You take that verse, and anywhere you will claim the promise of that verse—in your home, beside your bed, out on your job, wherever you are—the Lord has promised he will meet you and come into your heart.

When we speak of Christianity we are not talking merely about believing that someone named Jesus Christ lived two thousand years ago. We are talking about an experience with Jesus Christ which is personal in the here and now. So I said to him, "wherever and whenever you will receive the Lord and accept the promise of that verse, the Lord will save you. Several weeks went by, and I was coming in for the evening meal one night, and my wife said, "Some man wants to talk with you on the phone, and he is all excited. She called his name, and I didn't even remember the name. I picked up the phone and the fellow was all excited. He exulted, "You remember me. You remember me. I'm the guy you gave Romans 10:9 to. Well, preacher, it worked! Preacher, I got to rolling that Romans 10:9 over in my mind, and the Lord has been dealing with my heart about it for days now. I went to the factory where I work today and right down between two pieces of material, I claimed that verse. I invited the Lord Jesus into my heart, and it works." Yes, it does work.

When you meet the risen Christ there is *demonstration*. But when you meet the risen Christ there is also *dedication*. There has been a running debate as to whether Thomas actually took his fingers and put them into the prints on Jesus' hands and put his hand into the side of the Son of God. The other disciples must have touched Jesus. In Luke 24:38-39, Jesus gave the same invitation to them. In 1 John 1:1 John, who was present on that occasion when he saw and handled the risen Christ, states: "that which our hands have handled of the word of life." They had physical evidence that Jesus Christ was literally alive from the dead. But I don't think Thomas ever touched Him, because Jesus would have said, "Because thou hast touched me, thou hast believed." But Jesus said, "Because you have seen me." I think only one glimpse of those wounds of the Lord Jesus, one glimpse of the living Lord standing in front of him, dissolved his doubts and fanned his faith into a fire. That was enough. I do not believe he reached out with physical arms to touch the Son of God, but I believe he reached out with those two arms of faith and cried, "My Lord and my God."

What a confession! That is the greatest confession in the New Testament. That is the greatest statement any human being can ever make to the Lord—*my Lord,* confessing his sovereignty. Jesus Christ is the sovereign, the Lord. The question is not, do you believe intellectually that Jesus Christ is alive? The question is: have you received him as the living Lord in your life? Does he run your life today? "My God"—his Deity. This Jesus is God. Jesus didn't rebuke Thomas's statement of faith.

When Simon Peter went to the house of Cornelius they all fell at his feet, and Peter said, "Get up, I'm a man—not God." When the apostle Paul was preaching the Word of God in the city of Lystra the people thought he was a god, and they came out and began to worship him, and Paul tore his clothing and protested, "No, I am not God." But when Thomas fell before the Lord Jesus and said "My Lord and my God," he was not rebuked by the Son of God, for Thomas was confessing with his lips the fact that Jesus Christ was God on a cross. He was God in the tomb. He is God who lives forever as the living, reigning Lord. This brings us face to face with the statement from one of the greatest men of England, C. T. Studd. He was a wealthy man who was confronted by the claim of the Deity of Christ. Here is what he said, "If Jesus Christ be God and died for me, then no sacrifice is too great for me to make for him." Can you make that declaration of faith today? Can you say to Jesus Christ, "My Lord and my God"? Meeting the risen Christ leads to that declaration.

Number three, meeting the risen Christ leads not only to *demonstration* and *dedication,* but it leads to *declaration.* Jesus reached out into the centuries, and he said, "Thomas, you believe because you have seen: blessed are they that have not seen, and yet have believed." Do you know what he was doing there? In those words the Lord was pointing out the fact that, by personal experience, there are multitudes of people who have invited Christ into their hearts on the basis of faith, and their lives have been miraculously changed by him. There was a lawyer named Frank Morrison who didn't believe in the reality of the resurrection. He set out to write a book disproving the resurrection. He became confronted with indisputable facts of Christ's resurrection to the point that the result of his investigation was a book entitled *Who Moved the Stone?* It stands today as one of the most tremendous books proclaiming the resurrection of Jesus Christ. He is alive!

You see, I'm included in this verse. Jesus has pronounced the blessing upon my heart. I am included in those who have not seen and yet have believed. I have never seen him with these physical eyes, but I have the experience of 1 Peter 1:8 where it says, "Whom having not seen, ye love; though now ye see him not, yet believing, ye rejoice with joy unspeakable and full of glory." I can't explain it. I can't give you all of the definitions of it, but I can just simply testify that somehow, when I was a nine-year-old boy, though I had never seen Jesus with the eyes of my physical body, I believed on him in my heart, and Jesus came into my heart. He came into my life, and he has changed my life. I have never again been the same.

You ask, "How do you know he lived?" The chorus, "He Lives," goes: He lives, He lives, Christ Jesus lives today. He walks with me and talks with me along life's narrow way. He lives, He lives, salvation to impart. You ask me how I know he lives. He lives within my heart.

When the apostle Paul was laying out the appearances of the Lord Jesus he mentioned the five hundred, The Twelve, Cephas, James, and all the others. Then he declared, "And last of all he was seen of me." I want you to step in line with Paul and the rest of them and declare, "He was seen of me."

5.
The Young Ruler
(Who Wasn't Rich at All)

Mark 10:17-22

The Lord Jesus and the "rich young ruler" provide a remarkable contrast. Here were two young men standing face to face and heart to heart. One of these young men had great possessions. The other, the Lord Jesus, had left the possessions of heaven's glory and made himself poor to become our Savior.

One of these men had high position. The Lord Jesus left his position upon heaven's glory throne and entered this world to die. This story is the recounting of a tragedy. There was much that was right about this young man who came at the right time, for he came in the days of his youth or young adulthood. He came to the right person, for he came to the Lord Jesus Christ. He asked the right question, and he received the right answer . . . but he did the wrong thing.

Here was a young man who could have been in salvation's *Who's Who,* but instead he turned out to be in the Bible's *Who's Not.* It was a tragedy of a young man who met the Lord Jesus, who heard the plan of salvation, and yet turned away and did not follow the Lord. First of all, I want us to consider the *man,* and there are two thoughts I want us to see about this man. Let's consider the man and his quest. The Bible declares that this young man came to Jesus, and that he came running and kneeling. It was wonderful that the young man in those early years of his life came to the Lord Jesus. The Bible counsels young people to come to Christ. The youth age, the days of our maturation, are initial days. It is essential that you give your life to Christ at that time. Ecclesiastes 12:1

exhorts, "Remember now thy creator in the days of thy youth."

Wouldn't it be a wasted life to God? Wouldn't it be a waste to give the flower of your life to the devil, and then give the stem to the Lord?

Here was a young man on a quest. We discover, according to the Scriptures, that he was rich. There was certainly nothing wrong with his riches. His riches could have been used to bring honor to the Lord. His riches could have been used to help the cause of Christ on earth. The Bible also indicates that he was respectable. In fact, this young man was able to say to the Lord Jesus, "I have kept all of these commandments from my youth." He was well-thought-of; he was outwardly a moral person. We wouldn't minimize that at all. There is no virtue at all in living a polluted life. There is something to be said for the young person who determines that he is going to live a morally pure and clean life. This young man was respectable, and he had been recognized by the people in his community. The Bible relates that he was a ruler among the people. He was rich; he was respectable; but he was also restless.

The fact that we see him coming and kneeling to the Lord Jesus indicates that this is true. Somehow his riches had not been able to buy what was missing in his life. Somehow the position this young man had gained so early had not satisfied the deep longing of his heart. He was a young man who was looking for the missing ingredient. How picturesque of the lives of multitudes of young people today, young people who often have all that money can buy, young people who have prominence and prestige, and yet there is a restlessness in their lives. It required a great deal of courage for the young man to do that. The crowd in which he moved was probably hostile to the Lord Jesus. Some of his friends were perhaps even beginning to contemplate and to plot the death of the Son of God. And so it was with courage that this young man broke away from the crowd and knelt in the presence of the Lord. The young man and his *quest*.

Two, I want you to notice the young man and his *question*. He came to the Lord Jesus and implored, "Good Master, what shall I do that I may inherit eternal life?" He put his finger on the greatest question any person can ask. He was asking the way to heaven and how it is possible for a person to receive eternal life and go to heaven when he dies. Of all the questions that will arrest your attention and concern, none is so vital as the question of eternal life. I have an intuition that somehow this young man understood there was more to life than he had ever seen with his eyes, that there was more to life than he had been able to touch with his fingers. He was not asking here about the years of his life, but how to add life to his years. He was asking about this commodity of eternal life.

That was quite an admission on the part of this young religious leader when he asked the Lord Jesus what he must do to inherit eternal life. This young man was an expert in religious matters, considered one of the most religious people of his time, and yet he came to Jesus, and didn't know the road to heaven. It is rather tragic that many people have many answers in life, and yet they don't have the answer to the main question. Isn't it sad that there are people who train their minds to understand the technicalities of space travel, surgery, computers and calculators, and yet they are spiritually ignorant about the matter of eternal life. There are multitudes of people who know how to make a living, but they don't know how to make a life. We learned how to make a journey to the moon, but precious few people understand how to make the journey to heaven.

I think you have noticed immediately the flow in the question, for the young man asked, "What shall I do to inherit eternal life?" Those of you who are saved understand that you don't do anything to inherit eternal life. There are two basic opinions about what it takes to obtain salvation, two basic points of view as to what salvation is all about. A friend of mine told me about a lady who went to her doctor. Her doctor looked at her and in frankness he said, "Lady, I want to tell you that you are obese. In fact, to be perfectly blunt, you are fat," and she said, "Well, I want a second opinion." He added, "OK, and you are ugly, too!" Tact was not one of his traits. There are many people who teach that you get to heaven on the basis of what you are able *to do*. So there are people struggling and striving frantically, seeking to earn and to merit heaven. The Bible makes it clear that eternal life is not something you do. Eternal life is a gift which God gives in the person of his Son, Jesus.

The Bible in Romans 6:23 declares that "the wages of sin is death, but the gift of God is eternal life through Jesus Christ our Lord." God gives eternal life through his Son, the Lord Jesus. I want to illustrate how you gain eternal life. You see, if you want eternal life, God is saying, "I have wrapped up eternal life in my Son, the Lord Jesus." You accept Jesus Christ, and in so doing you receive eternal life. In 1 John 5:11-12 the Scriptures say, "And this is the record, that God has given to us eternal life, and this life is in his Son. He that hath the Son hath life; and he that hath not the Son of God hath not life." The young man had a flaw in his question. He was asking Jesus how to be saved, and yet he didn't understand that salvation is given to an individual in the Lord Jesus.

Now let's move onto number two, and let's consider for a moment the Master. Let's see how the Master deals in this interview with the rich young ruler. Now I observe two ideas about our Lord's dealing with this young man. First of all, I see our Master's *investigation*. In the words which Jesus addressed to the man, he was investigating the very depths of his heart. It is obvious from what Jesus said to the man that the young man was ignorant of two extremely important matters. He was ignorant about the person of Christ. For Jesus responded to the man and asked, "Why callest thou me good? there is none good but one, that's God." Jesus was probing the heart of the young man.

He was saying, in essence, to the man, "Young ruler, do you understand what you are saying? Do you understand the ramifications of calling me good?" Jesus was stating a fact here—that goodness resides in God alone. Jesus was saying you have only one of two alternatives. "You cannot call me good unless you call me God, and if you call me God, then you can call me good." What you believe about Jesus Christ and his person is vitally important.

But not only was he ignorant of the person of Christ, he was also ignorant of the purpose of the commandments. Jesus said to him in verse 19, "Thou knowest the commandments." Then he began to list some of the Ten Commandments, and the young man responded: "Master all these have I observed from my youth." I think outwardly this was true. So far as the outward keeping of the law and the morality of this young man's life was concerned, he probably did. But Jesus was investigating his heart, was going beneath the surface of his shallow goodness. The problem with this young man was that he had given himself only a casual glance. He had only superficially looked at his goodness and had determined that he had observed the law. This is the problem in our day. There are multitudes of people who casually glance at their outward goodness, and they determine that they are good, but Jesus carries us beneath the surface. Jesus wants us to probe our hearts and see where we really stand before him. There is a goodness which is so dangerous because it is so deceptive. Human goodness apart from Jesus Christ is the worst form of human badness. The Bible emphasizes that "there is none good, no not one," that "all have sinned, and come short of the glory of God." The Law had not done its work in the life of this young man. This young man had been satisfied with shallow observations, and he had never permitted the Law to do what the Law was intended to do. Some people have the idea that the purpose of the Ten Commandments is to give you a guideline to go by, and that somehow if you can make about a C or a C-, you will make a passing grade and that will get you into heaven.

A few years ago I was in a revival meeting in Central Georgia, and we visited the home of a man sitting on a big veranda. I sat there with the pastor of the church and talked to the man. The man said to me, "Well, preacher, my religion is the Ten Commandments. I just keep the Ten Commandments, and I'll depend on that to get me to heaven." It didn't take me long to go down the Ten Commandments and explain their deeper meaning and have that man admit that day that in spirit, if not in overt action, he had violated every one of the Ten Commandments. If you are depending upon your goodness and ability to keep the Ten Commandments to get yourself to heaven, then you don't have any more chance than an elephant on roller skates has of getting to the moon. You do not reach heaven by keeping the Ten Commandments.

The Bible teaches that the Commandments are like a mirror, and the purpose of that mirror is to show ourselves in need of a Savior. According to Paul, the Ten Commandments are like a schoolmaster. You see, that's what had happened to the apostle Paul. Some have the feeling that maybe this rich young ruler was the apostle Paul before his conversion. I doubt it, but I do think there is a rather interesting connection between what this man thought about the law and what happened in the life of the apostle Paul. Paul was like the young man. If you had asked Paul about the Ten Commandments, he would have averred, "I have observed all of these from my youth up." In fact, Paul wrote in Philippians 3, "Concerning the righteousness of the law I was blameless." There came a day, though, when the Spirit of God set the Law in front of Paul. It was like a mirror and Paul saw how far short he fell from the glory of God. At that moment the Commandments "slew" him, and he saw himself as a lost, undeserving, hell-bound sinner in need of a Savior. That is what Jesus was trying to do with this young man. If the young man had really understood the purpose of the Commandments, instead of saying "all of these have I observed from my youth," he would have said "all of these have I broken from my youth."

Let's move on. Look at our Master's *invitation*. Ah, verse 21 says, "Jesus beholding him loved him." I like that. When the Lord Jesus Christ saw this young man in all of his vigor and vitality, in his openness and desire to know about eternal life, it drew out the compassion, warmth, and love of the Jesus. Jesus invited that young man to follow him, and Jesus observed, "One thing thou lackest: go thy way, sell whatsoever thou hast, and give to the poor . . . come . . . and follow me." "One thing thou lackest." When Jesus said that, it was like wounding the Achilles heel of that young man. It was like pouring ice-cold water into his face. It was like puncturing the rising that was growing in his heart, for there was a hindrance in his life. There was something which was keeping this young man from receiving Jesus Christ as his Savior and his Lord.

You say, "Well, now, preacher, does that mean in order to be saved I have got to sell everything I have and give to the poor and then follow Jesus?" No, that is not the point at all. Jesus who looked into the heart of that young man saw his condition. He saw the one thing which kept the man from receiving Him as personal Savior. Jesus put his finger on that thing. But the principle is: you must surrender whatever it is that keeps you from receiving Jesus as your personal Savior. In his instance it was his riches. In your instance it might be a life-style, and it might be that Jesus would speak to you today, "One thing thou lackest. Give up that boyfriend you are living with and follow me." Or, in your case, sir, it might be, "Give up that illegal business deal you are engaged in and follow me." You see, different ailments demand different cures, and the Lord Jesus knows exactly why you are not saved. The message of Jesus to you is to separate from whatever keeps you from being saved.

Gipsy Smith, the great evangelist, was in a city for a crusade, and a young mother brought her small son to meet him after the service. She wanted her little boy to be able to say that he had shaken the hand of the evangelist. So she nudged the little boy up to Gipsy Smith and told Mr. Smith that she wanted her boy to shake the hand of the evangelist. Gipsy Smith bent over and said, "Good evening, young man." Timidly the boy said, "Good evening, sir." Then Gipsy Smith put out his hand and said "put 'er there," and the boy kept his hand behind him. His mother pushed him forward a little more and said, "Shake hands with him, shake hands with him," and the boy wouldn't do it. Finally she pulled his little hand from behind him and she instructed, "Shake hands with him." Then Gipsy Smith took the little boy's hand and pried open those fingers, and in the hand were three tiny marbles.

Jesus says, "One thing thou lackest. Whatever it is that keeps you from embracing me as your Savior, get rid of it and come follow me. Young person, would you like a challenge in your life. I know of no more thrilling and more exhilarating and more satisfying challenge in all of life than that of following the Lord Jesus Christ. When I was sixteen, having been a Christian since the age of nine, the call of Jesus Christ to follow him unreservedly and totally came to my heart. In obedience to the command to follow the Lord Jesus Christ he has led me into paths of prosperity, roads of blessings, and a life that is totally fulfilling. "Come follow me," says Jesus Christ.

Then there was the mistake. You see, it was decision time. The call of Christ had come to his heart. The Lord had exposed the hindrance in his heart. The Lord was challenging him and calling him away from his own "goodness" and away from his own possessions. The struggle was on. The young man began to breathe hard, and he wiped his forehead, and he bit his lip. The angels stopped what they were doing, looking over the battlements of heaven with hushed anticipation. The angel at the book of life poised the pen, ready to write the man's name up there, and the demons in the pit crawled up from what they were doing, looking in anticipation to see what the rich young ruler was going to do. Tragedy of tragedies, he made the mistake of mistakes. His mistake was: he was remorseful instead of repentant. Verse 22 states he went away "sad at that saying, and went away grieved."

The word sad occurs only one other place in the whole New Testament. It occurs in Matthew 16:3 where Jesus talked about the sky getting red and lowring of the sky. When the Scriptures say that this young man was "sad at the saying" of the Lord, it meant that his countenance fell, and that his face began to look like a thundercloud on a summer afternoon. He was filled with sorrow and remorse. He had heard the way of salvation but rejected it. The rich young ruler heard the way of salvation, found it hard, and went away with sorrow.

Your sorrow won't save you. Being moved won't save you. It is not enough to hear preaching. Maybe God has been bringing a turmoil inside of your heart, and there has been a spiritual upheaval going on within you. There is not enough grief in the human heart to make it saved. There is not enough sorrow to bring etermal life into your heart. It is not enough to be remorseful. The Bible declares that except you repent and turn around, you will perish. The man was remorseful instead of repentant.

He made a mistake because he chose the material rather than the eternal. Do you get the picture? He had rushed, filled with anticipation and emotion, to the feet of the Lord Jesus. He asked the right question. He got the right answer, and then he turned and went away because he had great possessions. The tragedy was not that he had great possessions. The tragedy was the great possessions had him. This man knew what he needed, but he wasn't willing to give up what he wanted. He needed God but he wouldn't give up his gold; he needed life but he wouldn't give up his luxury. He chose his riches, and he turned his back on the redeemer. He chose the material rather than the eternal.

Jesus asked, "What shall it profit a man if he gain the whole

world and lose his own soul?'' And the man walked away. I have
often wondered what happened. We really don't know. There is a
little hope in the word *grieved*. It could be that he went home and
that the sorrow in his heart worked into a godly sorrow that led him
to repentance, and later he received Christ as his Savior. I hope that
is true, and if it be true then the angels would have shouted with
joy, and the devils would have screamed out their scalding rage.
But it may have been that, when he went away and he reached
home he said, ''I can't imagine what happened today. I can't
imagine being so overcome with emotion. I can't believe it. I made
such a fool of myself in front of everybody, falling at the feet of
that rabbi from Nazareth, and to think how close I came. I almost
gave it all up. I almost followed this carpenter from Nazareth.
What got into me? But I am not primarily concerned about that
rich young ruler today. I am primarily concerned about you. You
have asked the right question. You have received the right answer.
You know the one thing you lack is Jesus Christ. You realize that
the need of your life, the answer to the problems that plague you,
and the solution to the dilemmas and the misery in which you find
yourself is to totally and unreservedly receive Jesus Christ as your
Savior.

What will you do? One thing thou lackest. That one thing you
lack is the main thing. It's the only thing. That's like saying to a
watch that has lost its main spring, one thing thou lackest; that's
like saying to a car without a motor, one thing thou lackest. That's
like saying to a body without blood, one thing thou lackest.

George Whitefield, the British evangelist, was holding a series of
meetings and was staying in the home of a well-to-do family. Because of the busyness of the meeting and the responsibilities which
were his, he didn't have the opportunity to talk personally with the
family about their relationship to Christ. So before he left his room
for the final day, on the window of the room he scratched these
words, ''One thing thou lackest.'' When the people came to clean
the room there was the message, ''One thing thou lackest.''

Oh, I pray that the Holy Spirit of God will etch upon the window
of your soul, ''One thing thou lackest.'' Reject whatever it is that
keeps you from Christ and come follow him.

6.
The Outcast
Who Became an Evangelist

John 4:1-30

In this touching passage we see how the Lord Jesus deals on an individual basis with a "down and outer." There is considerable help and instruction here for all of us as we seek to win people.

I am arrested by the statement that "Jesus must needs go through Samaria." There seems to have been a divine necessity placed on the Son of God. Jesus never did anything haphazardly. Every move Jesus made was according to a divine plan. On this occasion there was a woman in Samaria who needed to hear about the water of life, and so Jesus "must needs go" through there. When Jesus came to the familiar Jacob's Well, he sat down because he was wearied from his journey.

We notice here that Jesus Christ, who was God come down to mankind, was also a man and experienced what we do. Jesus became hungry and he ate food. Jesus became thirsty and he drank water. Jesus became so tired he sat down to rest. Jesus Christ was and is God of very God, but he was and is also man of very man. As man Jesus was able to understand the needs in the life of this woman's heart—as God Jesus was able to meet those needs. The Scriptures indicate that as Jesus was sitting at the well he heard footsteps. He turned around and saw the woman of Samaria coming with a waterpot poised on her head. There were traces of fading beauty in her face, but there were also evidences of sadness, emptiness, and disillusionment on her countenance. She was a woman whose life was filled with problems, many of them self-made, so the Lord Jesus, like a master surgeon, skillfully, carefully, and tactfully began to unravel the problems of her life. One by one by one he resolved the problems which she faced. Now Jesus Christ is the supreme problem-solver. It was an act of grace and mercy that Jesus the problem-solver should come along at exactly that particular time.

I want us to observe the manner of our Lord as he dealt with the problems in her life. First of all, I note that this woman at the well had a tongue problem. Now it's evident that she had that problem by the opening conversation between her and the Lord. Jesus made to her a most kind and gentle request. In our terminology, the Lord was merely asking her to give him a drink of water. It would help our understanding of what was taking place if we could catch the tone of voice and the emphasis in the response of the woman. In response to that simple request for water she said something like this: "How is it that you, being a Jew, ask a drink of me, a woman of Samaria?" The tongue problem of the woman indicated the prejudice and hostility of her heart. Her words reveal the historical prejudice in which she found herself.

Notice in verse 9 that the Jews had no dealings with the Samaritans. That was a situation which went back hundreds of years. When the Jewish people in the Northern Kingdom were carried away into captivity, the poorest and lowest of the Jews were allowed to remain in the land. During the processes of time those poor Jews intermarried with the Canaanites and others, and there emerged from that intermarriage a people known as the Samaritans. You can well imagine how the Jews felt toward half-breeds. You can envision the prejudice that was in their hearts when they returned to the land and found these people. So there was prejudice, animosity, and hostility between the two groups to the extent that the Samaritans wouldn't go down to Jerusalem to worship, but rather they had erected a rival temple at Mt. Gerizim. This woman was reflecting the prejudices of her time.

Now prejudice is certainly not new to our day. We are living in a society that is filled with many kinds of prejudices—not only racial prejudice but economic prejudice, social prejudice, and religious prejudice. The tongue problem of this woman revealed prejudice of her heart. But it also showed her own personal prejudice. She somehow had allowed her own heart to be gripped by the prejudices of the past. In her words of bristling hostility toward the Lord Jesus Christ, she indicated that she had lumped all of the Jews in one sack. She had a tendency to generalize. She believed that what she had seen about some Jewish people was true about all Jews, and often we make the same mistake, do we not? Sometimes we allow our personal prejudices to make us feel certain ways.

Isn't it wonderful to notice that the Lord gave no evidence whatever of any prejudice in his heart? I think that is one of the reasons the Scriptures stated that "Jesus must needs go through Samaria." Orthodox Jews simply didn't do it that way at all. If you can visualize for a moment how the land of Palestine was laid out, you will discover that down in the South was Judea. Above it was Samaria, and above that was Galilee. In order to travel from Judea to Galilee, the shortest and most normal route would be straight through Samaria. But Orthodox Jews wouldn't do that. They crossed over the River Jordan to the Eastern shore, went up the side out of the way, and then back into Galilee. But Jesus was different—no prejudices on the part of the Lord. So here he was dealing with a needy woman, a woman who had problems in her life. Jesus is always so kind and so patient. When she gave that snappy answer, I suppose if it had been you or me, we would have snapped back. Maybe I would have pushed her into the well, but not the Lord Jesus! He kept on tactfully and gently working with her, taking her where she was and leading her where he wanted her to be.

There is tremendous wisdom for our hearts as we think about telling others about Jesus Christ and winning souls to him. We need to accept people where they are, with all of their hang-ups and all of their prejudices, and lead them to the place they can receive the water of life. I heard about a barber who had recently been converted, and he was on fire for the Lord. He was ready on his job to win folks for Christ. So a little fellow came in one day, got into his chair, and the on-fire barber pulled out his razor strap and his razor. He raked it across the strap, and he said, "Brother, are you prepared to die?" The little fellow jumped up, ran out, and they never saw him again. Beloved, we need tact. We need to deal lovingly with the problems of life.

Second, the woman also had a thirst problem. She was coming to the well at noontime, and she was there to draw water from Jacob's Well. Jesus said some things which indicated her ignorance of living water and her interest in the same. Jesus said in verse 10, "If thou knewest the gift of God." She didn't know about the gift of God. She didn't realize that God wanted to give her a salvation that could completely meet the needs of her life. There are many people who are not aware of the gift of God. There are many who do not know that God freely offers them the gift of salvation. God wants to *give* you salvation. You can't earn it. You can't merit it. You certainly do not deserve it, and yet God wants to give you a gift. But the woman didn't know that. She also didn't know Jesus, for Jesus said, "If thou knewest who it is that saith unto thee." She didn't know who Jesus was.

She didn't understand the power of the Lord, and she responded to Jesus with "Sir, thou hast nothing to draw with, and the well is deep." She didn't understand the power of the Lord Jesus. Now part of what she said was correct. She said "the well is deep." That was certainly true. The last time I was in the Holy Land, we went to Jacob's Well, which is one of the few authentic sites in the Holy Land. The guides will take you to many places, and you're not sure if the places are genuine. But this is one of the places which is for real. Jacob's Well. The last time I was there one of the monks who was at Jacob's Well took a penny, dropped it down into the well, and we listened and we listened and we listened. Then finally we heard the splash far down in Jacob's Well. Some 120 feet deep is Jacob's Well. She was right about its depth, but she was wrong about the other. The well is deep, yes, but she said, "Thou hast nothing to draw with." She didn't understand the power of Jesus. She didn't know that he has access to channels of refreshment, grace, and glory that can bring the living water of life into an individual. Her ignorance.

Then Jesus made some statements that aroused her interest. You see, she was a thirsty woman. "Whosoever drinketh of this water shall thirst again" (v. 13). But I've got some water you can drink, and you will never again get thirsty. I believe you could put the words of Jesus in that verse and place them as a sign over every well this world has to offer the hearts of men. There are many wells men try. There are many places where people go seeking to find refreshment that their souls so desperately need. Solomon tried everything. Solomon tried many of the wells of this life. He tried the well of wealth, and it didn't satisfy the thirst of his soul. He tried the well of pleasure, and it didn't satisfy. He tried the well of lust, and it left him thirsty again.

So it is in the lives of every person who tries to find a well to satisfy the deep thirst of the human soul. "Whosoever drinketh of this well shall thirst again." So people continually come to their particular well in the ground. They continually try to drink from the broken cisterns of their own devising, which can really hold no water, and they forsake the Lord Jesus Christ, who is the fountain of living water. They come constantly without satisfaction. But Jesus remarked, "I want to tell you about a different kind of well, about something that can absolutely slake the thirst of your heart." Jesus said, "If you will take a drink of this water, which I offer you, it will be in you a well of water gushing up into everlasting life." Jesus was talking about salvation, the water of life. And, you know, I am amazed to see how Jesus used simple things to illustrate how simple salvation is. For instance, you remember one time Jesus talked about his being a door. "I am the door, if you come in you will be saved." How simple it is to go in a door. You open the door and walk in. That is how simple salvation is, if you want it. And here Jesus describes salvation as being like taking a drink of water. It will be like an artesian well down inside of you. It will be constantly gushing forth, and it will satisfy you the rest of your life. I have accepted the invitation of Jesus Christ, and I took that drink, and since that day my relationship to the Lord has indeed been a well springing up in my heart that has continually and lastingly fulfilled the deepest thirst of my soul.

She was interested in that. She begged, "Sir, give me this water"—I wonder if you are interested. One of the requirements in order to be saved is that you *want* to be saved. One of the requirements is that you want the water of life. Is there a concern in your heart? Do you have a thirst problem? Are you thirsty for something you have never found in your life? Not only did she have a thirst problem, she had a transgression problem. If I had never read this passage, I would have been totally unprepared for what Jesus did. I would never have expected the story to take this turn. Jesus said something that stiffened her as if she had been hit by a sudden blow. Jesus said, "Go call thy husband." Then she tried to conceal her transgression problem. She replied quickly, "I have no husband." She was unwilling at that point to face up to the transgression problem in her life, and she was desperately reaching for any kind of covering to conceal the sin problem in her heart. Folks are still doing that. We all do. None of us really want to face up to the transgression problem in our lives, and we use every means possible to conceal the real condition of our souls.

So people today put it off on "the new morality." "This is the new morality," and others try to cloak their sin by alibiing, "Well, this is just the times we live in." Others try to excuse their sin problem by saying, "Everybody else is doing it. It's natural for everybody to do it that way." She tried to conceal her problem, but Jesus absolutely made that woman confront her sin. Jesus with words of kindness, but words of truth, said, "You said the right thing. You don't have a husband. You have had five husbands, and the one you are living with now is not your husband." Jesus pulled away the cloak. She was able to see her heart and who she really was. I wonder what Jesus is speaking to us today. To the woman at the well Jesus said, "Go call thy husband." But for you he may be saying, "Go call thy wife whom you have offended." "Go call your child whom you have neglected." "Go call thy girlfriend whose purity you have stained." "Go call that businessman you have conned." "Go call that secret sin which gnaws like a rat at your soul." The Word of God exposes us, lays us bare. There is no place to hide. You can never drink of the living water until first you are willing to turn your back on those leaking wells of transgression where you have so often gone. She had a transgression problem.

She had another problem—a theology problem. What she did at this point was so typical if you have ever had much experience in witnessing to people on a one-to-one basis. You know what I am talking about. You witness to an individual, the Spirit of the Lord begins to convict them of their sin, their need of a Savior, and they are confronted with a decision for the Lord. Then they change subjects on you, and they "get religious." And they want to become "theological." That is exactly what she did. "Sir, I perceive you are a preacher. I want to ask you a question on theology." Now the town outcast becomes the town theologian, and she said, "Where do you worship? Where is the right place to worship?" And she brought up the age-old theological problem between the Samaritans and the Jews. She said, "We have a temple," and I can almost see her pointing to Mt. Gerizim that is right across from Jacob's Well. She said, "Our fathers say that there is where to worship." People are worshiping up there to this day. Some of the oldest copies of the Pentateuch in existence are housed on top of Mt. Gerizim. "Your church says that you have got to go down to Jerusalem to worship. Which place is right?" Now we hear this today. It's worded a little bit differently. A person comes face-to-face with the claims of Jesus Christ, and then they say, "Who is right—the Baptists or the Methodists, etc.?" "Why are there so many denominations?" "What about the hypocrites in the church?" I have a good answer I always give about the hypocrites in the church. "Of course, I know there are hypocrites in the church. I have to be their pastor. I know all about them. But I had rather come to church with a few hypocrites than to die and be in hell with all of them." Let God deal with the hypocrites in the church.

In his response to her, in essence he says "that the true worshipers worship God in spirit and in truth." It is not a matter of place. It is a matter of person. It doesn't matter where you worship. Listen, you can worship knee-deep in carpet with a program and elaborate chandeliers if you want to, or you can worship God under a brush arbor with sawdust on the floor. All that matters is that your soul worships God through the person of the Lord Jesus Christ. Then she proceeded a little further, "I know the Messiah is coming." Jesus, in essence, said to her, "The Messiah has come." She was looking for the Savior, and Jesus Christ said if you will look right at me, you will see that the Savior has come. The issue is the Lord Jesus Christ—the fact that Jesus Christ has come into this world, that he offers the water of life, that God says the only way you can come to him is through the person of the Lord Jesus

Christ. That is the question you have to settle now—what will you do with Jesus Christ?

She found herself face-to-face with Jesus. Of course, we know that the Savior has come. We are aware that after this point the Savior went to the cross and died there. We know that Jesus was buried in the tomb for three days and three nights. We affirm that on that Easter Sunday morning Jesus Christ rose from the dead, later ascended back to heaven, is at the right hand of the Father, and is also in the midst of God's people on this earth. All of this is true. We say to thirsty souls today, "Jesus Christ is the answer to every problem in your life."

A few years ago I was witnessing to a young fellow and at the beginning he said, "I am going to college, and I want to know about evolution. I want to know about evolution and the Bible. I want to know about all that." And I said, "You know that is a real, real good question, and I tell you what let's do. Let's take that question, and let's put it up here on the shelf for a little while, and let's talk about Jesus and your need of him. After we talk about that, we'll talk about evolution." We went right on through and shared the Word of God with him and the Scriptures about how to be saved. God's Spirit moved in his heart, and it wasn't too many minutes until he received the Lord Jesus as his personal Savior. After he was saved I said, "All right, now let's talk about evolution." He said, "Ah, forget it. I'm not interested in that anymore." You see how the Lord solves your problems.

The woman at the well was the town outcast. None of the other women evidently would have anything to do with her. She came at noontime, the hottest time of the day. No one else was there. The other women had come in the morning. They would return in the late afternoon.

She was the town's outcast. She had her waterpot, going to fill it again and again with the water at that well. When she met the Lord Jesus and received a good drink of the living water, she left her waterpot and went into the village. I have often wondered what happened to that waterpot. I wonder if they are trying to sell that waterpot somewhere in the Holy Land today. She left it. She left her interest in it. She had found another well and another water.

She ran back to her village, and she who was the town outcast now became town evangelist. She reported, "O come, come see a man who told me all things ever I did! Is not this the Christ?"

She had gone from the point when she called him a Jew. Then she called him sir. Then she called him a prophet. Now she called him *the Christ*. What do you call him? Are you ready to invite him into your heart? On the authority of Jesus' words, the water that he gives "shall be in you a well of water springing up unto everlasting life."

7.
Heat in the Kitchen

Luke 10:38-42

This passage of Scripture is set in a visit of our Lord to the village of Bethany, to the home of Mary, Martha, and Lazarus. Their home seems to have been a place where the Lord could frequently come for rest and relaxation. It was one of those rare places where the Lord could go and feel perfectly at home.

Probably all of us have had a place like that in our lives. There have been places in my ministry where I felt free and perfectly relaxed—totally at ease. I think that quite frequently after the busy activities of the day Jesus traveled over the Mount of Olives and into the little village of Bethany, there to visit at a home where he was welcome. I wonder if Jesus is at home in your home, if you in your own home have opened up your doors to him and have said, "Lord Jesus, you are welcome in this place." What Jesus did in the home of Mary and Martha, Jesus is wanting to do and will do in your home.

In John 11:5 the Bible tells us that Jesus loved Mary and Martha and their brother, Lazarus. In the experiences of joy Jesus Christ was often there. When sorrow came to this home he was there. And what Jesus Christ did in the home of these three, he is willing to do in our homes today. If we will open up our homes to him, he will dwell there. Jesus Christ will be the silent listener in every conversation. He will be the unseen guest at every meal. In the joys and in the sorrows Jesus will be there and will minister to our needs. This is a poignant passage from the Word, and it gives us one of the great interviews in Jesus' life. I want us to study this passage around three basic ideas.

Number one, I call your attention to the sisters in the home. In this passage Lazarus does not come into view, but Martha and Mary, the two sisters in this home, are prominently pictured. They were sisters by flesh and blood, but it becomes obvious that these two sisters were quite different in temperament and personality. What is true in the lives of human beings, so far as the family is concerned, is also true in the lives of the members of the family of God. When the Lord saves us and puts us into his family we are all different. We have different emphases, we respond to our Lord in different ways. I'm glad it's like this. The Lord saw to it. You are not like me and I'm not like you. I have a different approach to the Lord and you do, too. When the Lord saves us he doesn't make robots out of us, and he doesn't demand that we all be exactly the same.

There is an infinite variety among the people of God. God's people have different gifts, different means of serving the Lord Jesus, and so this is what we view in the lives of these two sisters, Martha and Mary.

When we look at Martha her work impresses us. Martha's way of expressing her love for Jesus was in the area of her work. She would show her love for him by what she did for him. It is quite significant that the Bible says (in verse 38) that it was Martha who received the Lord Jesus into her house. She opened the door of welcome to the Son of God. That speaks volumes about Martha. It is certainly something when a woman has enough love for the Lord to open up the door of her home and invite him in. She was the hostess of the house. But no sooner had Martha welcomed the Lord Jesus Christ than she was on her way into the kitchen, and she was busily making sure that the table was spread exactly right. She was seeing that the servants were on their toes and that they were doing the job. She was scurrying all around, tending to the various details of the kitchen. She was baking over here. She was broiling over here. She is cooking right there, for this was Martha's personality. All of us have seen Martha. She is practical in her personality. She thought: *I'll show my love for Jesus by what I do for him.* The Marthas among us are practically oriented, and they give themselves to a constant round of activities. The Marthas in our churches are those who can be depended on to serve on committees.

They will attend all of the meetings. They are constantly on the move.

Thank God for the Marthas in our church. Where would we be in our churches were it not for those with Martha-type personalities who are willing to do the nitty-gritty tasks that have to be done to perform the work of the Lord? Here was Martha with her strong point, work. But on the other hand there was Mary.

Verse 39 says that Mary sat at Jesus' feet and heard his words. The emphasis in the life of Mary seems to have been worship. Mary was sitting at the feet of Jesus Christ and learning of him. I have the idea that Mary was more contemplative in her personality. Mary thought, *I'll show my love for the Lord by spending time with him. I will get as close to him as I possibly can. I'll sit at his feet.* In those days, for a person to sit at the feet of another probably meant one of two things. It meant that they placed themselves at the feet as a learner or as a worshiper. Both were true of Mary. I think Mary realized who the Son of God was and what he had come into this world to do, and so she worshiped him as she sat at his feet. When I study the life of Mary I discover that every time Mary is presented in the New Testament, she is "at the feet of Jesus." Three times we see Mary there, and every time she is sitting at his feet.

You remember the apostle Paul (in Philippians 3:10) made this great statement, "That I may know him, and the power of his resurrection, and the fellowship of his suffering." Mary fulfills that desire, that threefold aspiration, of Paul. The first time we see her is in this passage here. She had come to understand how you get to know Jesus. Now how do you get to know Jesus? What is the secret of an increasing knowledge of Jesus Christ? We believe that the Living Word, Jesus Christ, has been revealed to us in his Written Word, the Bible, and we learn about Jesus Christ as we read the Word of God. I would like to encourage all of you to get your Bibles and begin reading through them. As you listen to the Word of God you will discover that you learn more and more about Jesus. You can't learn more about Jesus and not love Jesus more. Why, the more I learn about Jesus the more I love him. The more I learn of his interest in me the more I love him. The more I learn about what Jesus did for me, the more I love him. Mary's emphasis was sitting at his feet, listening to his word. I have the idea that on Monday morning, when washday came along, Mary would get her washing done, and then she would hurry off to hear Jesus teach the Word of God. Of course, Tuesday was "ironing day," and she would get her ironing done, and then hurry off to sit at the feet of Jesus and to hear his word. The apostle Paul said, "That I may know . . . the power of his resurrection."

In the eleventh chapter of John we have the account of the death of Lazarus. When Mary received the word that Jesus Christ was coming, even though belatedly she ran out to meet him. She fell at his feet and she cried, "Lord, if you had been here my brother wouldn't have died." Jesus answered, "I am the resurrection, and the life: he that believeth in me, though he were dead, yet shall he live." She learned the power of his resurrection at his feet.

The third time we see Mary at the feet of Jesus, she comes to know about the fellowship of his suffering. In John 12 we are told that Mary had saved up some expensive perfume, probably worth about a year's wages in the currency of that time. She took that expensive perfume and poured it on the feet of Jesus, and then she wiped the feet of Jesus with her own hair. There she was at the feet of Jesus, sharing the fellowship of his suffering. Mary had learned the secret of where to live. She had learned that she must learn to live at the feet of Jesus. There were the two sisters, so different and yet so vital. Martha worked. Mary worshiped.

Two, I want us to look at the scene in the home. They had a real "scene" there. It almost ruined the happy occasion. Get the picture. Here was Martha busily at work in the kitchen, and then right amid the party, Martha did something that came close to destroying the beauty of this experience. I see Martha as her brow is besweated. I see the frown on her face. I see her with a platter in one hand and with a pitcher in the other. All hot and bothered, she burst into the presence of Jesus, and they had a scene. Now look at Martha. I want you to see Martha three ways. First, Martha fretting. Verse 40: "But Martha was cumbered about much serving." The word *cumbered* there means she was distracted, and the word literally could be translated, "She was dragged about." The problem was that Martha was not handling the work, but the work was handling Martha. The work was causing Martha to be fretful. She was so busily engaged in working for Jesus that she found herself in a position of being distracted and dragged about. She was in danger of offending the very one she was working for.

I can almost see the situation. In those days they didn't have air-conditioned kitchens or microwave ovens either. They had little fires in the kitchen, and that fire of dried thorn bushes and camel's dung could be hot and uncomfortable. Perspiration was pouring from her body, and she was busy, busy. She was so distracted by her work that it became her greatest enemy. That is the picture of many Christians today. Read carefully, there are multitudes of Christians who are busily engaged in working *for* the Lord, but they are not spending time *with* the Lord. There are loads of Christians who are fretful, irritated, and aggravated in the very work they are doing in the name of Jesus Christ. If your work for Jesus is causing you frustration and anxiety, is distracting you and keeping you from fellowship with Jesus, then there is plenty wrong with the work you are rendering. There is no excuse for Christians to get irritated.

You say, "Well, preacher, are you setting yourself up as an example? Don't you ever get irritated?" Yes, I do but there is still no excuse for it. I shouldn't do it. Serving Jesus ought to be a joy. It ought to be a thrill to serve the Lord Jesus. My friends, if your work for Jesus has become a frustration, and you are fretful and irritable in your service for him, then there is something missing in your relationship to him. We Christians ought not to become fretful and irritated at home, should we? We can get irritated, and our words become sharp, and we put bad inflections on how we speak, and our irritability hinders our testimony at home. Sometimes that happens out in life.

I was with a good Christian man several months ago. During the course of the meal he became extremely demanding of the waitress. The coffee wasn't brought to him on time. He got very insulted. Then the food didn't suit him, and he sent it back two or three times. Oh, he was so irritable, and then when the meal was over he pulled out a gospel tract, gave it to her. And I said, "Oh, my soul, don't do that!'' What kind of testimony is that for a Christian when we are irritable and hateful and do it all in the name of the Lord? There was Martha fretting.

But I want you to look at Martha, not only fretting but also Martha resenting. She was filled with resentment. I see Martha as she came to the door and looked out there. She saw Mary sitting at the feet of the Lord, and resentment boiled up in her heart. She said to herself, ''Why, of all things, would you look at my sister? I have all this work to do back here in the kitchen, and there she is sitting at the feet of Jesus, not helping me at all. So she burst in on the Lord and said (in verse 40), ''Lord, don't you care that my sister has left me to serve here alone?'' She was resentful toward Mary. She was implying that her sister wasn't doing her part. I do not believe Mary was shirking her responsibility. I believe that Mary was doing her part, for we may have missed a word in verse 39. ''She had a sister called Mary which [here is the word] also sat at Jesus feet. Do you see the implication of that word also? Mary sat at the feet of Jesus also. It means that Mary had already done her part in the kitchen. Mary was not only a worshiper, she was also a worker. The problem was not that Mary hadn't done enough work for the Lord. The problem was she had not done enough work to please Martha. The problem was Martha. I think Martha had an Elijah complex, I really do. Martha thought she was the only one. Martha thought her manner of serving Jesus and loving Jesus was the only way you could do it, and what she was resenting on the part of Mary was that Mary didn't come in and stew with her. Martha felt her own importance and felt that what she was doing for Jesus was so important that Mary's part was not important at all. That's the way many react today. She was resentful against her sister. She was resentful against Jesus. Look at her. She asked, ''Lord, don't you care?

I recall the disciples of Jesus hollered that one time as they were out on the Sea of Galilee, and a great storm came up. Jesus was asleep in the ship, and the disciples rushed to where Jesus was sleeping. They shook him and yelled, ''Master, carest thou not that we perish?'' Don't you care? Now we may never have put it in those words. We may never have expressed it exactly that way, but I have a feeling that all of us say that to Jesus sometimes. When we get so busy working for Jesus and we become fretful and filled with anxiety sometimes we really say, "Lord, don't you care? Lord, doesn't it matter to you?" We forget 1 Peter 5:7, "Casting all your care upon him, for he careth for you." Of course, he cares. Does Jesus care? "Yes, he cares. I know he cares. His heart is touched with my grief. When the days are weary and the long nights dreary, I know my Saviour cares." There is Martha resenting.

Then Martha was dictating. Did you notice that Martha called Jesus "Lord" and then proceeded to tell him what to do? "Lord, bid her come help me." Many of us do that sometimes. We want to tell Jesus how to solve the problem. Martha's solution to the problem was more activity. Martha wanted to solve the disturbance in the home by making Mary get just as active as she was. To become just as fretful as she was. The tendency for overactive Christians, Christians whose sole response to Jesus Christ is to do something for him, is to increase what they are doing. I believe that one of the dangers facing modern Christianity is that we have the idea that all we have to do in our relationship for Jesus is just work, work, work. If we can go to enough meetings, and if we can get enough study-course awards, and if we can be on enough committees, and do enough things, then somehow we are going to win the approval of Jesus Christ. It doesn't work that way. So a scene was going on in the home.

Number three, the solution. Jesus is so tender. Jesus is so kind. Jesus spoke to her, "Martha, Martha." I can feel the compassion there. Oh, there is a mild rebuke there, but it is certainly not what I would have done. Do you know what I would have done? I would have said, "Look here, Martha, you moron, you get back in that kitchen. You are as wrong as you can be, and you get in there and shut the door and also shut your mouth." That is what I would have done.

Two guys were talking about which sister they had rather marry, and one of them said, "Well, I think I'd like to have Martha before dinner and Mary after dinner." The other one said, "No, I think I'll take Mary all the time, because to eat a meal prepared by one as irritated and as fretful as that would certainly not be very tasty." I think probably I'd take Mary all the time too. But Jesus was kind. He said, "Martha, Martha." And so Jesus solved the problem. How does Jesus go about solving the problem?

Number one, he calmed her anxiety. "Martha, Martha, you are careful and troubled about many things." That word careful is our word "anxious." The same word Paul used in Philippians 4:6, "Be careful for nothing; but in every thing by prayer and supplication with thanksgiving let your requests be made known unto God." Jesus was saying, "Martha, you are so easily worried. Martha, you are so worried about so many things."

Did you know that most of things we worry about never come to pass. I was reading the other day that if you would make a list of all the things that you worry about, and the things that you don't worry about, you will discover that most of the things you worry about never come to pass, and most of the things you don't worry about do come to pass. So why worry? But most of us do. I was reading this week about Archbishop Trench, one of the great New Testament scholars, and his *Synonyms of the New Testament* are terrific volumes, but the Archbishop for some reason got this morbid fear that the limbs of his body were going to become insensitive so he would lose all feeling. He became obsessed with it. One night he was sitting at an elaborate state dinner, and he blurted out, "Oh, it finally happened. It's finally happened. I haven't got a bit of feeling in my right leg," and the lady sitting next to him said, "Your grace, if it will be any comfort to you, it's my leg you are pinching!" We worry about things that never happen.

He said, "Martha, Martha, you are so filled with anxiety, and you are in such turbulence about so many things." Guess what Jesus did? He simply spoke the word, and he calmed her anxiety. That is what you need, fretful Christian. That is what you need today, busy Christian. You need to hear the word of the Lord Jesus, taking the anxiety out of your heart. Listen to Jesus. "Come unto me, all ye that are weary and heavy laden, and I will give you rest." Listen to Jesus Christ. "Peace I leave with you, my peace I give unto you: not as the world giveth give I unto you." He speaks his word, calming our anxiety.

Second, he corrected her activity. Jesus said, "Martha, thou art careful and troubled about many things, But one thing is needful: Mary has chosen that good part.'' And the word *part* there is related to a Greek word that is sometimes translated fellowship. ''Martha, your sister Mary has discovered the secret of priority. Mary has discovered how to put worship and work in the proper order.'' Now the solution to Martha's problem was not to cease her activity. That is the mistake of the deeper-life movement. The deeper-life approach to the whole situation is stop all activity, quit coming to the services. Don't be so legalistic as to attend all the services of the church. Don't dare go to the stated visitation time— that is legalistic. The extreme approach to the deeper-life movement is to go home, sit down, and let the Lord do it all. I've got news for you. You can sit home and let the Lord do it all, but if you don't get up and go to the kitchen you will starve to death! The solution to Martha's dilemma was not to cease her activity. Jesus Christ didn't tell her to stop doing what she was doing, but rather Jesus pointed her to putting things in the proper order. Mary had discovered the priority. Mary understood that work must proceed from worship.

My friends, our activity is only a ministry as it flows from our relationship with Jesus Christ. If you are busy coming to the services, if you are busy attending meetings, if you are busy serving on boards, if you are busy visiting and doing all of your activities, yet you are not daily meeting Jesus Christ—sitting at his feet, listening to his word—you are destined to become a frustrated, fretful Christian. And we must learn to choose that ''good part.'' ''One thing thou lackest'' is God's word to the sinner, but God's word to the saint is, ''One thing is needful.'' Needful above all things is a vital personal fellowship with Jesus on a daily basis. In John 15:5 Jesus said, in essence, ''If you abide in me, and I in you, you will bear much fruit, for without me you can do nothing.'' You will discover that when you sit at the feet of Jesus, learn his word, and let Jesus speak to you, you develop a personal walk with him. Then you will see that your work for him will be the natural outflow of your personal walk with him. The message is not to stop what you are doing. It is not to resign from the committee, not to resign your

Sunday School class, but to fall at the feet of Jesus. That is the one thing that is needed.

Did it work? I think it did. Turn to John 12:2. In the passage of Luke 10 there were probably four people present; Mary, Martha, Lazarus, and the Lord Jesus. Martha was serving for four people, and she was "cumbered about," all filled with frustration and anxiety, serving four people.

But when you come to John 12, on the basis of parallel accounts in the Gospels, it seems that the twelve apostles were there, plus Jesus. If you count Simon the leper, there were at least seventeen persons there for that occasion. Seventeen people, and yet read verse 2, "There they made him a supper and Martha served."

No frustration, no anxiety, no turbulence. Why? Martha had learned the secret of serving as a result of closer fellowship with Jesus Christ. May God help us to learn to sit at the feet of Jesus . . . and then serve Him.

8.
Condemned No More

John 8:1-11

If you have a modern version of this passage, you have probably noticed in the margin or somewhere close a little statement that these verses are not found in the "oldest and most reliable" manuscripts. In fact, some editions of the Scriptures put these first eleven verses at the conclusion of the Gospel of John and make it clear that the oldest manuscripts do not record these eleven verses.

There seems to be no debate, however, about the fact that these verses record an occurrence which actually took place in the life of the Lord Jesus Christ. There is something here that is true to the character of the Lord and is so much like him in his dealings with individuals that there can hardly be any question that what is recorded here is an experience that actually occurred. Jesus was known as a friend to sinners when he walked on this earth. These verses give us the truth that Jesus was exactly that, that no one was beyond the reach of his love and compassion.

In Luke 19:10 Jesus said, "The Son of man is come to seek and to save that which was lost." So Jesus Christ walking in this sinful world came in contact with individuals who needed his mercy, his grace, and his love. Our hearts are blessed as we view the lovely Lord Jesus sinless, and yet coming in contact with sinful individuals to change their lives and to make them what God intended them to be.

The woman in these verses is an unnamed woman. She has not been given a name as if the Word of God politely veils over the record of this sinful woman, but she was a woman who had a soul, a woman who had a heart that needed to be changed. She was an individual for whom Jesus Christ had come to seek and to save. I marvel at the infinite grace of the Lord Jesus. I wonder at the marvelous release of Jesus Christ in the lives of individuals that can remove them from a sinful past and give them a Christ-filled future.

So I want us to look at this experience of our Lord as he interviewed the woman who is known as "the condemned woman." To help us understand the passage a little better, I have organized our thinking around several points. Number one, I want us to think for a little while about the *accusation*. There was an accusation made by a group of men concerning this woman. I would like for us to feel the atmosphere and the picture in the passage as it is presented. In verse 1 we are told that Jesus had spent the night on the Mount of Olives, and then early in the morning the Son of God came to the Temple, he sat down, the people gathered around him, and he began to teach them. Such teaching this world has never known, such truths this world has never heard as the literal Word of God poured from the lips of Jesus, and so it was an early-morning Bible teaching experience. The crowd had gathered to hear the Lord when there was heard a commotion coming toward the Lord. There was a crowd of angry men shouting, and there was commotion around a woman as she was pushed into the presence of the Lord.

So rudely did they come into the presence of the Lord. So callously did they handle this woman; as we look at her we see a woman in trouble. Her hair was disheveled, her garments were torn. Upon her face there was sullenness, defiance, and rebellion. This woman had been brought into the presence of the Lord Jesus by the scribes and Pharisees. Now the scribes and Pharisees in the days of Jesus were the self-appointed custodians of public morality. They took upon themselves the prerogative of determining the behavior of individuals. They were the ones, if they so desired, who put the finger of condemnation on an individual. They were the ones who determined what the common standards of public decency were. So these men brought a woman to the Lord Jesus, and they hurled their accusations against her.

The accusations were very serious. The Bible relates that she had been taken in adultery, caught in the very act. There was no heresay about it. It was not a matter of idle gossip—it was absolutely known. Their accusations were absolutely true. We know, of course, what the Scriptures say about this. We are aware that the seventh of the Ten Commandments teaches "thou shalt not commit adultery." There is no question about the sinfulness of her act, no condoning of what this woman had done. She was guilty of a scarlet sin, a terrible act, and all through the Word of God there is a uniform condemnation of the sin.

In Hebrews 13:4 the Bible says, "Marriage is honorable, and the bed undefiled, but whoremongers and adulterers God shall judge." So there is no question about her guilt, no question about the truthfulness of their accusations. We are now living in a time of liberalized views concerning sex. We are living in a time when there is an attempt to minimize the truth and the absoluteness of God's standards, and in a very real sense this particular sin has come to be *the sin* of our day. Whereas God makes it a dreadfully serious matter, people have sought to minimize the impact of this sin. Everywhere around us this sin is being glorified and flaunted before the public. I think there are many reasons why this liberal trend has arrived in our day. I think the impact of our music, our pornography, our movies, and our indecent attire have contributed to the air of laxness concerning God's commandment, "Thou shalt not commit adultery," and no society can survive a lessening of its moral standards. Rome was wrecked because of laxness concerning this sin, and America cannot survive a collapse of its moral standards.

A few years ago I read a book by Dr. Howard Marcuse, and at that time he was a professor in one of the colleges in California. He was a philosopher of the radical left in our country. The book was entitled *Eros and Civilization*, and in that book he proves that no society can survive a disintegration of its moral standards, and, of course, he was saying that this is one of the ways to destroy our society, and to cause America to collapse. There are forces at work in every area of our society which are seeking to undercut the standard of God concerning the decency of the home, the purity of the body, and the decency and the morality of marriage. So we are confronted with a very serious sin.

I would not for a moment minimize what this woman had done, and she had absolutely been caught. Friend, "Be sure your sin will find you out." Folks may laugh at sin, may minimize its importance, but it is a written truth of God that somewhere along the road sin catches up with an individual. The Bible says, "The wages of sin is death." The Scriptures say, "God is not mocked, for whatsoever a man soweth, that shall he also reap." There is probably no sin recorded in the Bible that brings such definite results as the sin of immorality. It pays off its deadly toll bodily, mentally, and spiritually.

Here is a woman who was caught in the act of adultery. Not only was she caught, but she was condemned. These scribes and Pharisees had read their Bibles, and they had read it well, and they had carefully underlined those passages that suited their own end. Back there in Deuteronomy 22:23-24 there is a definite command of God that those who were caught in the act of adultery were to be carried out of the city, and they were to be stoned to death. That sounds pretty severe, doesn't it? That sounds like a stringent penalty for God to say that this sin deserves punishment by stoning. The point is that God is trying to illustrate his unchanging attitude toward sin. God loves the sinner. God loves you and me. We are sinners, and God loves us, but the Bible is clear when it teaches that God hates the sin in the life of the sinner, and the good news of the gospel is that God has sent his Son, the Lord Jesus, into this world to put sin to death on the cross, and to release the sinner from the power of that sin.

She was a condemned woman. She was under the condemnation of the law, and if they did what her accusers said should be done, they would have at that moment stoned her to death. Those men were interested in making an accusation against the woman, but also their accusation was moving toward another person, for they were primarily interested in accusations against the Lord. Now that is clear in verse 6 if you will look at it carefully. "This they said, tempting him [that is, Jesus] that they might have to accuse him [Jesus]." You see, the point of the matter is, they were trying to get something on Jesus Christ. They didn't care about that woman. So far as they were concerned she was a nobody. That woman to them had no name. She had no heart. She had no feelings, no emotions. She was a nothing—she was merely a pawn in their game. They were using this woman merely as a means to hurt the Lord Jesus. As you read the rest of the Gospels, you will discover there was what I call a get-Jesus committee. In other words, there was an unofficial committee of people who had decided they were going to "get" Jesus Christ. They couldn't stand Jesus. Jesus Christ was infinite purity walking around in a human body. He was absolute holiness walking on an unholy earth, and these religious pretenders and hypocrites who pretended to be what they were not couldn't stand the presence of Jesus Christ, so they organized a get-Jesus committee.

They said, "We will get him in trouble with the Roman Empire. We are going to ask him whether it is lawful to pay tribute to Caesar, and either way he goes we have him in trouble." And so they came to Jesus and asked, "Is it lawful to pay tribute to Caesar?" and Jesus implored, "Do you have a piece of money?" He said, "Let me see it." He took that piece of money and he asked whose image was that on the piece of money. They answered, "It's Caesar's," and then Jesus completely stunned them. He said, "All right, you render to Caesar that which is Caesar's, and to God that which is God's." When they got back into their "after-meeting," they said, "Well, that really blew up in our face, didn't it? We had better try something else, and so the get-Jesus committee decided what they would do. They would go down into the red-light district of their city, and they would find one of the ladies of the night plying her trade and bring her into the presence of the Lord, and they would impale him on the horns of a dilemma. They would quote for him what the Law had to say, and then they would get him either way he went.

If Jesus said that the woman should be released, then they would say, "Why, he doesn't observe the Law of Moses, and he is lowering the morality of our land." On the other hand, if Jesus had said, "Let her be stoned to death," then they would have said, "Some friend of sinners he is," and so they thought they had the Lord trapped. The accusers had now ushered her into the presence of Jesus. They could barely restrain their glee. They were smirking underneath their pompous ecclesiastical robes, for they had brought this woman accused before Jesus, and in reality they were accusing him, but now the story moves on.

Not only do we see the accusation, but we also see the *examination*. As I read the Bible, if I had not read all these passages before, I would be constantly amazed and surprised. The Lord Jesus just overwhelms me every time. He never does what I think he would do, and he always does exactly what he ought to do. The Lord Jesus took in the scene, and he saw this poor, sinful, condemned woman. He was aware of the crowd, and they were all looking on with baited breath, wondering what he was going to say, and then he completely reversed the situation on the accusers. Instead of examining the accused he examined the accusers. Wasn't that just like the Lord? And so I see his examination in two things.

I see it first of all in his *writing*. The Bible states in verse 6, as they were presenting their charges against this woman, that Jesus stooped down and with his finger wrote on the ground as though he heard them not. There are obviously two questions that come from these verses. One, why did Jesus stoop down? There are many possible explanations for that. Some have suggested that Jesus stooped down to hide the holy indignation and the burning shame that leaped to his face amid such a situation, and others have commented that Jesus Christ stooped down out of a sense of grief and modesty over the callous manner in which they brought this poor woman before the public eye. Question number two is, what did he write? For the Bible says that Jesus with his finger wrote on the ground. You will search the New Testament through, you will read all of the four Gospels, and everything you can about the life of the Lord, but this is the only time you will ever read that Jesus ever wrote anything. There is no question but what he could write. He had been brought up under the rabbis at the local synagogue in Nazareth, but this is the only time the Bible indicates that he did write. Isn't that a paradox, the Lord Jesus, so far as we know, never wrote a book, and yet more books have been written about the Lord than any other person and any other subject in the history of the world! Jesus Christ never composed a book that appears on the shelves of any library in this land, and yet Jesus Christ has been the theme of the greatest literature of all the ages. Jesus Christ is the principal character of the greatest songs that have ever been composed, and that emanate from the prolific pens of our best composers. Jesus Christ, the simple, humble carpenter of Galilee, never wrote another time so far as we can discover. What did he write? Wouldn't you like to know. And wouldn't I like to know? The truth of the matter is, "Not a one of us knows."

There are interesting suggestions. There are some who believe that Jesus wrote out the Ten Commandments as they were pressing him, and that is an intriguing conclusion because we do know that, when Moses went up on the mountain with two empty tablets of stone, Jesus, who is the incarnate God, took his finger out of heaven, and with his finger wrote upon the tablets of stone the Ten Commandments. It could be that right now Jesus is writing the Law as if to say to them, "You remind me of the Law. Why, my fingers wrote that Law. I stooped down out of heaven to give my eternal Law concerning right and wrong. You remind me of the Law. Yet Jesus Christ not only stooped down from heaven to write the Law on the tablets of Sinai, but the New Testament teaches that when we receive Christ as our Savior that this same God stoops into our hearts, and he writes the Law of God in our hearts, and he puts his truth in our souls, and he gives us the power to fulfill the requirements of the Law in the person of the Lord Jesus through the power of the Holy Spirit. He could have been writing the Ten Commandments.

There are some who claim he was writing the sins of the men who were condemning the woman. And the word used here is quite a word. It means to write down as a record against someone, and it could very well be that Jesus began to write the names of the sins of those men who were condemning that poor, sinful woman. We do not know what he wrote, but there was something about his writing that examined the hearts of these men. But not only did he examine them by his writing—he examined them by his *words*. They kept pressing the issue. Verse 7 says they continued asking him. They thought they had him. In other words they said, "All right now, Lord, you tell us. Come on, come on. Let's hear your answer. What are you waiting for? You're biding your time. We've got you, haven't we? Come on. What do you have to say?" What the Lord Jesus Christ said to them was like a thunderbolt out of a clear sky. They were utterly unprepared for what Jesus had to say. Jesus Christ stood, looked at them, and said, "Okay, he that is without sin among you let him first cast a stone at her." Brother, they weren't ready for that. They had come to condemn a poor woman from the lips of Jesus, and instead of hearing the lips of Jesus condemn the woman, they heard their own hearts condemning them.

Jesus said, "All right, I'm going to set up the criteria for judgment. I am going to fix the qualifications for the accusers. I am going to establish the requirements for the executioners. All right, you want to condemn her? You want to keep the Law? Here are the requirements—you must be absolutely without sin. The first one of you that is sinless, you pick up a stone and throw it."

I was sick one day watching television, and Dr. William Holmes Borders, the great black preacher in Atlanta, was preaching on this passage. He came to this part here ("Let him that is without sin, first let him cast a stone at her"), and he said, "If a one of them had thrown a rock at that woman, the Lord would have turned the heart of that rock into rubber, and it would have bounced back and burst their brains out!" And that is exactly the way I feel about it. "He that is without sin, let him first cast a stone." Let me ask you a question. Who was the biggest sinner? Was it this poor woman that had been caught in the act of adultery or was it these scribes and Pharisees and all of their religiosity and all of their hypocrisy? Friends, when you read what the Lord Jesus Christ has to say about it, you will discover that our Lord's most severe words were not to those individuals who had been caught in the clutches of their own sensuality, not those individuals who had been ensnared in the shackles of their own flesh, but the severest words of Jesus Christ were to those people who were guilty of the sins of disposition, the sins of jealousy, and the sins of envy and the sins of gossip and the sins of hate and the sins of pride. Those were the worst sinners, and some of you sit in our buildings so sanctimoniously, and they feel so holy and so righteous, because they have never been taken in the act of adultery. Yet, the Lord Jesus says to everyone today, "He that is without sin, let him first cast a stone."

Those words of the Lord Jesus will put you out of the rock-throwing business for the rest of your life. You will never be able to throw a rock at anybody. I think this is one of the funniest incidents in the Bible. I feel sorry for folks who never see humor in the Bible. I see a lot of funny places in the Bible. There are some items that break me up, and this is one of them. You get the picture. Here were these scribes and Pharisees. They had on all their phylacteries and their long robes with the broad rims. They were just so holy, and they knew how to talk and they knew how to pray their flowery prayers, and here they were in utter condemnation of that poor scum of a woman. Jesus said, "All right, you are going to condemn her. If there is a one of you with no sin in your heart, you cast the first stone, and I hear the dull thud of the rocks. And then they got in a line single-file, and the oldest of the lot lead the line. Do you know why he led the line? He had lived longer than the rest of them. He had sinned the most! That just breaks me up. That is a scream, but you see, that is the way our Lord examines us.

These men thought they had come to a lynching party. Instead they had come to see themselves as they really were, and they had come face-to-face with the condition of their own hearts, and probably for the first time in their own lives they saw themselves as God saw them. Have you ever seen yourself as God sees you? I mean when the facade is taken away, I mean when the veneer is peeled from your life, I mean when the mask of hypocrisy is removed from you, and you see yourself as you actually are. I have a feeling that if some of us could see ourselves as we actually are, instead of leaving sanctimoniously and piously from our buildings, we would prostrate ourselves on our faces at the altar, and we would not leave until we had heard that the Lord had forgiven us of our sin.

So there is the accusation, there is the examination, and three, *the liberation*. That religious crowd was gone. The folks who had gathered to hear the Lord Jesus were still there, but they were breathless and wondering what was going to happen next, and the Lord Jesus was alone with the woman. I have a feeling that, just for a little while, there was a pause. There was nothing said, and I think that pause was to give this woman a few minutes to become aware of how desperately she needed the forgiveness of her sins. She was a sinner in the presence of the Son of God. Here she was incarnate impurity in the presence of incarnate Purity. Here she was, the guilty one in the presence of the sinless One. Here was one under condemnation, and here was One offering salvation. Then I notice how my Lord Jesus deals with this poor sinner. I see how my Lord reached out to a woman stained by the filth of her own sin, condemned by her religious superiors. I see my Lord as he reaches out to her with a word of tenderness, and he said to her, "Woman, where are these thine accusers. Hath no man condemned thee?"

It touches my heart when I am aware that the word Jesus used for her is the same word that he used for his own mother when he was on the cross, "Woman, woman." The crowd wouldn't have called her that. You and I wouldn't have called her that. We would have had more damning words to use in describing her, but Jesus Christ has a way of calling things that are not as though they are. Jesus Christ looked at that woman, and he saw her not as she was, but as she was going to be by his forgiveness and grace. "Woman, where are these thine accusers?" You see, sin couldn't change the character of our Lord; nor could it freeze the fountain of his compassion. I don't know what you have done. I don't know how deep you may have sunk into the slime of sin. I don't know about that, nor do I care, but I know there is nothing you have ever done that can keep the Lord Jesus from reaching out with a word of compassion for you. By this time there was a change coming over her. Her face had lost its sullenness. Her countenance has lost its defiance. There was now a ray of hope in her eyes. There was now a little flicker of faith kindling in her heart. I can almost hear the quiver in her voice, and I can see the trinkle of the tears down her face as she replied to the Lord Jesus, "No man, Lord." Then Jesus reached out to her with a word of forgiveness: "Neither do I condemn thee." Ah, you say, "Preacher, was Jesus condoning her sin?" No. "Well, why is it, preacher, that Jesus could say to her, as sinful as she was and as deserving of judgment as she was, why could Jesus say to her, 'Neither do I condemn thee'?"

That is another reason why Jesus stooped to the ground. I think the great reason was that he felt afresh the burden of the load of the sins of the whole world. You see, the reason Jesus Christ can say to a sinful heart, "Neither do I condemn thee," is because two thousand years ago at a place called Calvary, the Lord stumbled up that hill, not only with a rugged piece of wood on his back, but the accumulated burdens of the sins of the world, and when they put him on that cross and hung him between heaven and earth, Isaiah said the "Lord hath laid on him the iniquity of us all." Has it ever dawned on you what it cost Jesus to say "neither do I condemn thee"? Listen, my friends, your salvation is free, but it is not cheap. It cost something. When Jesus can say to your heart, as he did to her heart, "Neither do I condemn thee," remember he makes that statement at a terrible cost by becoming sin for us at Calvary. When you read Romans 8:1 and rejoice in it as you should (where it says "there is therefore now no condemnation to them which are in Christ Jesus") rejoice in it. But don't stop there. Read the third verse where it says, "God sending his own Son, in the likeness of sinful flesh, and for sin condemned sin in the flesh." *Neither do I condemn thee.*

Note the order. That's salvation. "Neither do I condemn thee." That is the word of forgiveness. That is salvation. But then he said, "Go and sin no more." In some circles today they have it all different from that. We have cheapened salvation so much and made it such an easy "believism" in our day that if you rephrased it the way it is taught now, some folks would put it like this, "Neither do I condemn thee. Go and sin some more."

But Jesus not only gives a word of salvation. He gives a *word of sanctification.* I love that line in "Rock of Ages" where it says "be of sin the double cure, saved from wrath, and make me pure. That is sanctification. I'm talking about a salvation that saves and also gives a new dynamic, a new power on the inside that will help you to go into a life of peace and pardon and purity. It just changes your life.

I can almost picture her as she walked away, can't you? No longer the condemned woman. Now the cleansed woman. She walked away just as pure as the driven snow. She walks away just as pure as she were a baby upon the breast of her mother. She was a brand-new individual. She had the word of her Lord. *I am not condemned. I'm forgiven. I've got a brand-new life.* A few years ago I preached on this passage of Scripture and I got an anonymous letter. I normally don't read anonymous letters. I do read some. I have a funny book that I am preparing, and I take all kinds of stuff like that, and I put them in it. I have a feeling that when I get 65, it will be a scream to read this stuff, but I received this anonymous letter, and I had preached on "Neither do I condemn thee." The letter writer said, in essence, that she was a lady who was a member of our church, and she said, "Preacher, many years ago I was a lady of the night. I worked as a prostitute, and I realized that I was a sinner. I received the Lord Jesus Christ as my Savior, and he has changed my life, and now through the years I have tried to live for the Lord and to be a clean, pure person, and you will never know what it did for me and meant to me when you told me that our Lord can say, "Neither do I condemn thee. Go and sin no more." She said, "What a difference it makes in my life!" My friends, I don't know who you are, and I don't know what sin has hold of your life. I don't know what guilt is dragging you down and holding you, but I give you the words of Jesus, "Neither do I condemn thee."

I have often wondered how it will be when we enter the gates of heaven. I somehow imagine maybe the angels will be there to greet us as we come in, maybe with some word of encouragement. I can almost imagine as we go into the gates of pearl, and the angels are there to encourage us, I can hear one of them as he announces "enter and labor no more." And then another one cries out "enter and suffer no more." And another one says, "enter and weep no more." But I think the sweetest of all will be the one who says "enter and sin no more!"

9.
Salvation in the Death Chamber

Luke 23:39-43

The personalities of this Scripture found themselves at the point of no return, the ultimate extremity of life. These three were not on "death row," but they were in the death chamber on a hill called Calvary. Three men were crucified upon crosses. One of those men was a thief on the right side; the other on the left side was also a thief. The Lord Jesus was in the middle.

My last sentence is an accurate depiction of what the Lord Jesus Christ is and where he stands in every generation. Jesus Christ is indeed in the midst. He is the inescapable Christ. He is the unavoidable Christ, for Jesus is in the middle of our history. When we pick up a newspaper and read the date we see again that Jesus Christ is in the midst. When we write a check and date that check "in the year of our Lord," we are acknowledging that he is indeed in the midst. The question, of all questions, is, "What will you do with this Jesus Christ." Three men were on crosses that day; like grim scarecrows they were suspended between heaven and earth.

In that morbid setting we have the account of one of the most sensational conversion experiences ever recorded in sacred history. Here was a man who in his dying hour gave a demonstration of a remarkable faith. There is probably no greater demonstration of faith recorded in all of the New Testament. Here was a man whose past life gave no evidence of faith, and yet in those dying moments his faith was remarkable to the extent that the Bible has recorded it. There was an example of the mercy of Jesus Christ to the man who called upon him for salvation. That dying thief was the first trophy of God's grace at Calvary. The dying thief was the firstfruits of the work of Jesus and His salvation at that cross. I want us to look at the interview of our Lord as he spoke to a dying thief on the cross. We consider these verses around two major themes.

First of all, we look at the *appeals* of the criminal and then the *answer* of the Christ. You may not have noticed as you read this passage that both of the thieves on both crosses made appeals to the Son of God. This is a rather arresting thing to me. Both of these men were in the same straits. Both of them experiencing the same circumstances—they were both equally near the Lord Jesus Christ. Both of them heard Jesus speak, and they saw Jesus on his cross. Both of them were in need of forgiveness. Both of them needed the mercy of the Lord, and yet one of those men died *in* sin and went to hell; the other died *to* sin and went to heaven. That is one of the great mysteries of life to me. I don't understand how two individuals can come to a service, be in the same church, hear the same songs, hear the same sermons, and yet one heart is moved unto salvation, and the other leaves the building unmoved, untouched, and unblessed.

Somehow in the mystery of the way God has made mankind, somehow in the free-moral agency which God has deposited in humanity, have the right to say yes eternally or no eternally to the Lord. So these two men made their appeal to Jesus. Now one of the thieves made an appeal for rescue. We are told in verse 39 that one of the "malefactors which was hanging there railed on Jesus," that is, he rebuked Jesus, and he yelled, "If thou be the Christ, save thyself and us." Now we could say that was the normal eruption of a depraved heart. I think that was in part true on that occasion, for there was a man who was dying the way he lived. He had no room for God in his life; he had no regard for God; he had no interest in the welfare of men in this life. In death he died railing, rebuking, and blaspheming. But where did that man hear such words as this, "If thou be Christ"?

As you study the scene of Jesus Christ being crucified, you will pick up similar words from the people who gathered around the cross. The people derided and scathingly rebuked the Lord Jesus, and screamed, "If thou be the Christ, save thyself and come down.'' Religious rulers coaxed Jesus, "Jesus, if you are who you say you are, come down from that cross.'' The soldiers spoke words similar to those, for the Scriptures say they said, "If thou be the king of the Jews, save thyself.'' But I believe reflected in all of their words was a more sinister voice, the voice of Satan himself. You see, all through the life of the Lord Jesus Christ, Satan attempted to get Jesus to avoid the cross.

When Jesus was carried into that wilderness temptation experience, the devil said to him, "If thou be the Son of God, then take these stones and command them to be turned into bread; if thou be the Son of God, cast thyself down from the temple.'' The devil was seeking at the very outset of Jesus' ministry to get him to avoid the necessity of the cross. All through his ministry, and then at the moment when Jesus was in the death chamber impaled upon that rugged tree, the voice of Satan through this thief was again speaking, "If you are the Christ save thyself—come down from the cross.'' Don't misunderstand what the thief was saying here. This was not request on the part of that thief for salvation. He was not asking to be saved from his sins; he was rather asking to be spared from the punishment he was experiencing.

A. T. Robertson, the brilliant Greek scholar, said that what you have here is really an appeal on the level to escape prison. What the thief said was, "Let's break out of this situation. If there is anything you can do to get us out of this, do it right now because we are dying. I think that is an apt illustration of what a lot of lost people do. There are many people who would like to get out of the punishment that results from their sins, but they are not primarily interested in being saved from their sins by repentance and having a changed life.

A few years ago I worked with a young man who got himself in trouble with the law. He had been in trouble with the law on numerous occasions, but now it seemed as if surely he would go to prison. So he called for me and wanted to talk with me about salvation. I was happy to talk with him about it. I read the Scriptures to him and showed him what he had to do to be saved, how you have to repent of your sins and believe on the Lord Jesus Christ. He bowed his head. He supposedly prayed to receive the Lord. The next Sunday he came to the services and walked down the church aisle, joined the church, and I baptized him, but just as soon as the word came that he was not going to prison and was not going to suffer pumishment for his crime, he never came back to the church again. There was no interest on his part in spiritual things. Many people want to get out of the difficulty they are in, but not out of the depravity that is in their hearts in a salvation experience with Jesus Christ. Here was an appeal for rescue. "Save thyself and us. Come down from the cross."

But the other thief made an appeal to be remembered. Matthew tells us that, at the outset of this situation, both of the thieves entered into the railing against the Lord Jesus. At the beginning of the matter both of the thieves were involved in the rebuke, but somewhere along the line something transpired in the heart of this other thief. I don't know what it was, but I can use my imagination. Maybe you can use yours. As this thief was bearing his cross behind the Lord Jesus, as they were going toward Calvary's hill, I think this thief must have observed the actions and words of the Lord Jesus. The women alongside the road began to weep for the Son of God. Probably that thief began to think, *I wonder if anyone is going to weep for me.* And then he heard the stunning words of the Lord Jesus. Jesus said to those women, "women, weep not for me, but weep for yourselves." He had never heard a man talk like that man, and then he saw Jesus as they carried him up on skull hill, and he saw the calm demeanor of the Lord as he allowed himself to be nailed to that cross. In stark contrast to his own blaspheming, spitting, cursing, and efforts to escape, he had never seen a man face death like this man Jesus did. Then he heard the prayers of the Lord Jesus as Jesus prayed, "Father, forgive them, for they know not what they do." Father, forgive them. He had never heard a man pray like that.

Over the Lord Jesus there was an inscription which read: "This was the King of the Jews." That small inscription became a little Bible which preached to the thief that the One on the middle cross was more than a mere man. He was a King who had a kingdom. I believe that the Spirit of God in the death chamber began to work on the heart of this thief, and he turned to the other thief and began to speak for Jesus Christ. As you read the words of this man you are amazed at his knowledge of theology. It is remarkable what this man understood and believed just moments before he went out into eternity. This man understood reverence for God. He asked, "Dost thou not fear God? Reverence for God is the beginning of knowledge. The Scriptures say that "the fear of the Lord is the beginning of knowledge." When a person comes to understand that God is the creator, that mankind has been made in the image of God, and that he has a personal responsibility and accountability to God, he has made the first step on the road to salvation.

But he also understood the theology of judgment. He said, "Do you not see that we are in the same judgment," the same condemnation. He had come to believe in the principle of judgment. The business of judgment has been written into the moral order of this universe. It is true that God has so arranged this universe that every deed will be brought into judgment. God has decreed that the wages of sin is death. God has decreed that every sin shall be brought into judgment. Your sin will have to be judged somewhere. Your sins will either have been judged in the person of the Jesus Christ, or you must bear the blunt of the judgment of God upon your sins. The thief came to believe in judgment. He had also come to believe in his own sinfulness. He said to the other thief, "We receive the due reward for our deeds." That was quite an admission. This man was willing to admit personal responsibility for what he had done. It's not often you get folks to do that today, is it? It's not often folks are willing to say, "I'm the culprit. It's my fault. It's my sin. I'm to blame." You will never be saved until first of all you come to understand that you are personally responsible for your sins, and that you personally need a Savior to forgive you of your sins, and so he said, "We receive the due rewards for our deeds."

He also had come to believe in the sinlessness of Jesus. He said, "This man hath done nothing amiss," and the word amiss in the Greek language was a word which meant "out of place." "This man hath done nothing out of place." We cannot say that, can we? I can't say I have never done "nothing" out of place. That is not good grammar, but that is what I meant. I can't say that, and you can't say that. Too many times we have said things out of place, we have done things out of place. Too many times there have attitudes in our hearts that are out of place. But this man understood the absolute sinlessness of the Lord Jesus Christ. He came to recognize that there was a man dying on that middle cross who had done nothing worthy to merit that kind of judgment and punishment. That man Jesus Christ was totally sinless. The thief was a prime target bound for salvation. Here was a man who was ready to experience the salvation that Jesus died on that cross to purchase, and so he turned from speaking for Jesus and now spoke directly to Jesus. The Bible says that he asked in verse 42, "Lord, remember me." The tense of the verb at the beginning of verse 42 is imperfect tense which means action in past time going on. It meant repeated action, and so this was not just one time that the thief made this plea, but he made it over and over again. It was not just an arrow shot toward heaven, but it was a storm that bombarded the gates, and it echoed, "Lord, remember me, Lord, remember me, Lord, remember me." In the very requests of this man in the appeal for remembrance there was a beautiful picture of the marvelous grace of God that is revealed in salvation.

Now look at the *simplicity* of it, "Lord, remember me." Too many want to take salvation, make it difficult and hard to understand. Sometimes we preachers are guilty of that; sometimes the theologians want you to be able to articulate the formula exactly right, but if you really want to be saved, if you know you are a sinner and if you know that Jesus Christ died on the cross for your sins, you don't have to worry about how you say it. The Lord is so anxious for you to be saved that if, in your heart of hearts, you want to come to the Lord Jesus, you just put in any kind of word you want to, and the Lord will hear and he will answer. Jesus said, "Him that cometh unto me I will in no wise cast out."

Look at the simplicity of it, but I want you to notice the *singularity* of it. He said, "Lord, remember me." Not my brother, not my mother, not my sister, but it's me, O Lord." Salvation is a very personal matter. You say, "Preacher, my daddy was a deacon." Well, thank God for that, but your daddy can't save you. You say, "Preacher, my momma was a Sunday School teacher. Thank God

for that, but she can't save you. You must come to the point in
your life that you appeal, "Lord, remember *me.*" It is a very personal experience between you and Jesus.

But I want you to notice, not only the singularity and the simplicity of it, but note the absolute *sincerity.* Here was a man in
death row. The punishment had already begun. His life's blood was
pouring onto the ground at the bottom of his cross. He didn't have
time to play the hypocrite. He didn't have time to impress anybody.
He was facing eternity, and so in sheer sincerity he cried out to
Jesus, "Lord, remember me when thou comest into thy kingdom."
This beautiful picture of the salvation of this thief at the very gates
of death refutes many false ideas about salvation. This is one of the
greatest passages in the Bible not only to teach clearly what salvation is, but also to teach what salvation is not. This refutes the idea
that salvation can be earned by good works. Some people say,
"Well, I want to do good works. I want to earn my salvation. I'm
going to live a good life, and I'm going to treat my neighbors right,
and I'm going to pay my bills, and I'm going to do good works.
This knocks that in the head. You see, he wasn't able to do any
good works. He couldn't go out and rectify any wrong that he had
ever done. He was completely helpless. He was nailed to a cross. He
couldn't do any deeds of mercy. His feet were nailed to that cross.
He couldn't walk anywhere to live a good life in front of anybody.
This illustrates to us that we are not saved on the basis of what we
are able to do. The Bible says, "For by grace are you saved through
faith; and that not of yourselves: it is the gift of God: Not of works
lest any man should boast."

It refutes the idea that baptism saves. Now baptism is good. I
think it is good to be baptized. I believe that baptism, though it
does not confer salvation, *confirms* salvation. I think that it is the
answer of "a good conscience toward God," and I have always had
a problem understanding how a person can say, "I have received
the Lord Jesus as my personal Savior, and yet now I'm not going to
do what Jesus says and I'll not be baptized in obedience to him."
That doesn't make much sense to me, but you don't have to be
baptized to get to heaven. I like what that country preacher back in
Georgia used to preach. He said, "I'll tell you, bless the Lord, you

can be baptized in every ole frog pond in Georgia till every frog knows you by your first name, but till you get born again you are not going to heaven." The thief couldn't be baptized. Someone says, "I think what you have to do to be saved is live a good, moral life." Well, that is important, too, but living a good, moral life is an evidence of your salvation. It is not a means to your salvation. This passage refutes many of the false ideas people have about salvation.

This man simply pleaded to Jesus Christ for mercy, and the Lord heard him and the Lord answered him. Now someone raised the question, "What about deathbed repentance? Pastor, doesn't this teach deathbed repentance? Doesn't this teach that you can be saved right there at the moment of death?" Well, I do believe that it is possible for a person to be saved right at the moment of death. I know that none of us deserve to be saved at any moment in our lives, and a man on his deathbed who lived a wicked life doesn't deserve to be saved, but I didn't deserve to be saved when I was nine, but somehow God in his grace and mercy will save us anytime we call upon him. I want to point out, though this passage teaches that deathbed repentance is possible, I want to impress on you the fact that deathbed repentance is not probable. It is not likely that you are going to repent and be saved on your deathbed. Someone said, "One thief on the cross was saved that none might despair, but only one that none might presume." What makes you think you are going to have the opprotunity to be saved at the moment of your death. You might be killed instantly in a fiery car crash. You might be in a coma for days and days on a hospital bed somewhere. You may lose your rational faculties of thought. You may not have the opportunity to repent on your deathbed. Don't presume upon the possibility that one day you will repent just before you slip out into eternity.

An old preacher was preaching on the danger of procrastination and urging people to be saved while they had opportunity and the moving of the spirit in their hearts, warning people against the dangers of procrastination. Some wag in the congregation stood up and said, "Well, what about the thief on the cross?" and instantly the old preacher replied, "which thief?" Don't presume you are going to have an opportunity to be saved in such a manner.

There comes a time, I know not when, in the destinies of men that a person's eternal destiny is determined for heaven or hell. Don't think you are going to have an opportunity at the last moment. So here were the appeals of the criminals. One made an appeal for rescue. The other made an appeal to be remembered.

Let's look at the answer of the Christ. I marvel at the Lord Jesus. Here was Jesus Christ in the death chamber. He was impaled upon a cross, and yet he was in total charge of the whole thing. Here was the Lord in death, lingering on skull hill, and yet he was in total command. Jesus Christ decided to die on that cross. Jesus said in John 17, "No man takes my life from me. I lay it down." When Jesus died "he gave up the ghost, and he prayed, Father, into thy hands I commend my spirit." See now the word of the Lord.

First of all Jesus gave a word of affirmation. Look at the first word Jesus answered to the man. In the King James verson it is the word, "verily." In the Greek text it is the word, 'amen. Immediately you recognize the word 'amen transliterated into the English language is amen. Did you know that is one of two words in the world that is the same in every language. Two words are the same in every language, amen and hallelujah. You can be halfway around the world, and you can meet a believer anywhere, and if you don't know a thing about their language, all you have to do is say amen, and they can respond, hallelujah. And when Jesus Christ was on that cross, and when that thief appealed to him to be remembered, the Lord gave him a word of affirmation, 'amen. There was the picture. There had been two appeals made to the Lord Jesus.

I think when the Lord Jesus Christ was faced with that awesome alternative, the angels in heaven must have held thier breath. I think the saints of the Old Testament in heaven, on credit waiting for Jesus to cast that check on the cross, must have looked on in anxiety. Why, they would have to leave heaven if Jesus came down from the cross, and all heaven was looking, and Jesus Christ was faced with that eternal alternative again, but now it was much more intense. The pain was severe that he was going through. He was on the outskirts of hell. The hot flames of hell were beating upon him. One said come down; the other said go into your kingdom. What would be his answer? In the midst of that terrific dilemma the Lord Jesus Christ responded with a word of affirmation, amen. Do you know what he was saying? He was saying amen (So be it) to your salvation and mine. He was saying amen to the agony of the cross; he was saying amen to the plan of God for his life; he was saying amen to the possibility of the salvation of every soul that would ever be born. He responded with a word of salvation, amen.

"Today shalt thou be with me in paradise." That's a word of salvation. I love that word, *today*. That's God's word, today. Satan's word is tomorrow. As you read this book you may never have received the Lord as your Savior, and yet the Spirit of God is dealing with your heart. Perhaps you are right at the moment when you must make that decision, and the Spirit of God says *today,* but Satan whispers in your ear, "Tomorrow, tomorrow, put it off till tomorrow." But the Word of the Lord to you is today. "Now is the accepted time," says the Scripture. "Today is the day of salvation." *"Today,"* said Jesus, "shalt thou be with me." This Bible teaches an instantaneous salvation. The moment you repent of your sins and put faith in the Lord Jesus Christ, that is instant. You pass from death unto life; you pass from darkness into light; you pass from hate into love. "Today shalt thou be with me." Look at that. That's salvation.

Did you note in the passage that "with me" comes before "in paradise"? Salvation is a person before it becomes a place. "With me." Salvation is a personal experience with the Lord Jesus Christ. The word of salvation, but then there is a word of consummation. "Today shalt thou be with me in paradise." Where was paradise? The word paradise occurs only three times in all the New Testament—2 Corinthians 12:9 where Paul talks about the experience when he "was caught up into paradise and heard things which are not lawful for a man to utter." The third time is in Revelation 2:7 where the Lord Jesus says, "To him that overcometh will I give to eat of the tree of life, which is in the midst of the paradise of God." Before the resurrection of the Lord Jesus, the abode of the dead was referred to in the Old Testament as *sheol.* The New Testament rendering is *hades.* So the abode of the dead was *sheol, hades.* There seemed to have been two compartments to this abode of the dead, and the wicked dead went into the compartment which we call *gehenna,* but the righteous dead went into that compartment which we call paradise, but when the Lord Jesus died on the cross and was buried in the heart of this earth, a change occurred. Jesus Christ went down into paradise and announced liberty to the Old Testament saints, and Ephesians says "he has led captivity captive." Do you know what Jesus did? He emptied paradise and carried it into the very presence of God and the throne of God with him. When a person dies now, because of the resurrection of Jesus Christ, he goes to be with Jesus. Far more than the streets of gold, as marvelous as that may be far, more wonderful than the gates of pearl, heaven to me is *where Jesus is.*

And that thief heard the Lord say, "Today you are going to be with me." I heard about a doctor who was explaining to one of his patients about heaven and trying to describe heaven. He was reaching and grabbing for words, and in an effort to explain it he heard a scratch on his office door. He opened the door and in scurried his little pet dog, and the doctor said, "That's the way it is. My little pet dog knew I was in here. He didn't know anything about the room. He didn't know how it was decorated, didn't know about the pictures on the walls, or any of the decor. All the little dog knew was that his master was in this room, and that is where he wanted to be, and that is the way heaven is." I don't know all about paradise, I don't know how it's going to look; I don't know about the beauties and the glories that are going to be there, but I know that paradise is where Jesus is. When the repentant sinner will say, "Lord, remember me," that instant he gets the word of consummation, "Today shalt thou be with me in paradise." To be absent from this body is to be present with the Lord. In just a few hours Jesus was dead. The soldiers came with mallets and crushed the legs of the thief and he was dead. There he was—broken, bruised, crushed, and dead. That is what sin, Satan, and self did to him, and that is what it will do to you. It was all over for him, wasn't it? Or was it?

For somewhere that very day in the paradise of God there walked a redeemed sinner, arm and arm with a Savior who had said, "Today shalt thou be with me in paradise."

"The dying thief rejoiced to see that fountain in his day. And there may I, though vile as he, wash all my sins away."

10.
Heartwarming Along the Road

Luke 24:13-35

I have in my study a painting which means a great deal to me. The title of the painting is, "The Disciples on the Road to Emmaus." It is a picture of these two disciples of the Lord and Jesus himself as they walked together and talked together on the road to Emmaus. These two disciples were not a part of the original twelve of our Lord, but they seemed to have been a part of that larger group of men who had followed the Son of God.

In John 6:66 the Bible says that Jesus began to present some of his hardest sayings, and from that time many of the disciples turned away and walked with him no more. But among that larger group of disciples there were some who had stayed all the way to the crucifixion, and these two Emmaus travelers were included in that number. These disciples had stayed for the crucifixion, they had seen the Lord Jesus Christ nailed on the cross of Calvary, but they had not seen the empty tomb. These men knew the facts of the resurrection. They had heard the news that the women had gone to the tomb and that the Son of God was not there. They knew that the tomb was empty, but the facts and the reality of the resurrection had never gripped their hearts. I believe that these two disciples were very much like many of God's people on the Sunday after Easter. There are many who know that Jesus Christ is alive; they accept that fact intellectually, but the reality of it has never gripped their hearts.

Paul in Philippians 3:10 expresses the desire that ought to be the desire of us all when he wrote, "That I may know him, and the power of his resurrection." The resurrection of Jesus Christ is not merely a fact to be accepted, but it is to have an impact in our lives on a daily basis. These two disciples are like Christians today. They were in desperate need of a heartwarming experience with Jesus Christ. These disciples had the facts, but they lacked the fire. They had theology, but they lacked doxology! These men were in desperate need of an experience with Jesus Christ that would move and warm their hearts. I want us now to consider this experience when the two disciples walked on that road, and the living Son of God came to reveal himself to them.

I call your attention, first of all, to the divine conversation. The Bible reads that while these men were talking about the events that had occurred in recent days that Jesus Himself came and walked with them, engaging them in conversation. Jesus as he talked with them, from their lives the things that were bothering them. In this divine conversation we notice that their faith was *shaken*. You will note in verse 19 what they said concerning Jesus as a prophet. They were talking about Jesus in the past tense. They were talking about a conviction that had been theirs, but a conviction that now had been shaken in their lives. There had no doubt been a time when these two men had great faith in the Lord; their hopes had been lifted and their conviction had been strong that Jesus Christ was indeed the Savior of the world and that he would do everything he had promised he would do. They had seen the miracles of the Lord Jesus, and their faith had burst with strong conviction from their hearts. They had heard the teachings of the Lord, and their faith had grown as they heard him. They had been with the Lord Jesus just days prior to that time when they had entered in triumphantly into Jerusalem, and their faith had mounted wings and had soared.

But then came the cross of Calvary; then came the terrible scattering of the disciples, and they were no longer sure. Their faith was shaken. There are many people whose faith has been shaken. Somewhere along the way we have lost our ability to believe. Somehow in our days of skepticism and unbelief we have allowed the truths that are most precious and the convictions we thought we believed stronger than life itself to be shaken and to be disturbed. Our world is not so sure anymore.

Our world has placed its faith in technology and it has failed us. We have placed our faith in the politicians and they have disillusioned us. We have placed our faith in "religions," and we have discovered that all of them are dead-end streets. Our faith is shaken. I heard one time that the president of Harvard University made this statement, in essence, "The whole world is searching for a song to sing and a creed to believe. I think that is exactly right. Our world today is in desperate need of something it can trust, of something in which it can place its utter conviction and concern. Here were these disciples, their faith shaken.

Too, I notice here that the hope was shattered. For they said in verse 21 as they talked to Jesus, "We trusted that it had been he [Messiah]." Actually the emphasis here is the word hope. They were saying, "We had hoped that it would be he." Now they had lost their hope. They were not so sure that Jesus Christ was who he said he was. Now there had been a time, I believe, when hope had been strong in their lives. Their hope had been real, but if Jesus Christ were dead as they suspected he was, then their hope was shattered. They had hoped that Jesus would give them forgiveness of sin, but if Jesus were dead they were still in their sins. They had hoped that one day they would have a message that could be delivered to the peoples of the world, but if Jesus were dead, then their preaching would be in vain. They had hoped that they would somehow have an answer for the terrible dilemma of death, but if Jesus Christ were dead and still in that tomb, then the Bible said they were of all men most miserable. Don't you believe that the condition of these disciples is the picture of many disciples in our day? Many of God's people have allowed their hope to be shaken and shattered. The circumstances of life and the realities of the things that have come into the lives of people have caused them to lose their hope. Thus, we are living in a world of pessimism and despair, a world that has the idea that there is no better world, that death comes and there is nothing beyond.

I think our world is aptly pictured in the story I heard of the men who were in a submarine that went down. Divers dove in around the submarine, and they began to listen to the messages that were being tapped by the people inside of the submarine. As the message came out, it said "Is there any hope?" And the divers around the submarine tapped back, "There is none." Our world is saying, "Is there any hope?" and the messengers of doom are saying, "There is none." The disciples had a heartwarming experience with Jesus Christ that recovered their hope, but here they were sad of countenance. They were desperate men.

As I look at this story again I discover that their love was also stifled. As you read what they said about Jesus here, you cannot miss the fact that they truly loved Jesus. I can imagine as they walked on that road back to Emmaus, they must have remembered the day when they had walked to Jerusalem, and they had heard about this one named Jesus. They had heard what Jesus was doing. When they met him and walked with him for sometime, it was not difficult for them to love him. They had seen Jesus as he gave sight to blinded eyes, and it made them love him for it. They had seen the Lord as he caused crippled men to dance with joy, and they loved Jesus for his healing power. They had seen Jesus take boys and girls who had died and recover them to their grieving parents, and they loved a man like Jesus who could bring such hope back to the hearts of people.

They saw Jesus as he took an interest in people, and I think that is one of the reasons that these disciples had followed Jesus Christ. Jesus saw in them what they could become by the power and grace of God. All of us remember the tragic story of the People's Temple in Guyana. I have done a great deal of reading and have tried to discover why Jim Jones had such an attraction. One of the things I learned is that Jones had a way of causing people who followed him to think that they were important to him. He made them feel like they were somebody. He made them somehow feel there was a purpose for their lives. Here was a man who made people feel important to their suicides. But Jesus was one who reached down into the lives of men and women and challenged them to be what they could be by his power and love. They loved the Lord Jesus, but their love had become stifled.

We have seen the divine conversation, but as we move a little further in this passage, we also see the divine *confrontation*. As Jesus listened to them talk, he began to confront them with the condition of their hearts. Look at what Jesus says in verses 25 and 26 to them. Jesus said to those two disconsolate disciples, "O fools, and slow of heart to believe all that the prophets had spoken." That was exactly their problem. They believed some of the prophets, but they didn't believe all of the prophets. Those disciples had a way of doing what you and I do when we read our Bibles. They saw the things they wanted to see, and didn't see the unpleasant things they didn't want to see. They had read the prophecies that the Messiah would indeed be one of majesty, and that he would sit upon a throne of glory, and they had latched onto those prophecies and had believed them. Yet, they did not believe everything that the Scriptures had predicted the Savior would be and do. The cross had been very difficult for them. Jesus said, "Slow of heart to believe all that the prophets had spoken," and then Jesus began to confront them with a threefold truth.

One he confronted them with prophetic truth. Beginning in verse 27 he began at Moses, and in all of the prophets and in all of the Scriptures he expounded unto them the things concerning himself. That must have been a wonderful experience, don't you think? Can you imagine how that must have been as Jesus shared Scriptures which showed them pictures of himself. All of the Bible points to the Lord Jesus. In a real sense of the word we can say that the Bible is a *him* book. Jesus Christ is the central figure. Jesus Christ is the main personality. All of the pathways of the Scriptures ultimately lead to the Son of God. The Bible is like a vast art gallery in which there are many different pictures of the same personality.

I heard about a little chapel in the Italian Alps that has an unusual arrangement of statues. Down the inner walls of that chapel are statues of the Old Testament prophets, and all of those prophets are pointing toward the focal point of the little chapel, and there in the center of it all is a picture of Jesus himself. Whoever designed those statues in that chapel understood the foundational truth that all of the Old Testament points to Jesus Christ.

When you read your Old Testament you discover that all of it points toward the coming of the Son of Man. He began at Moses, Genesis, and he took them on a tour all through their Bibles, and he showed himself to them in all of that. Consider for a little while how Jesus Christ is revealed in your Bible. Why, in Genesis, Jesus is the promised Seed. In Exodus, Jesus is the Passover Lamb; In Leviticus he is all of the offerings combined in one. In Numbers, Jesus is the Star out of Jacob; in Deuteronomy Jesus is the Prophet who is greater than Moses; In Joshua, Jesus is Jesus; in Judges, Jesus is the Savior; in Ruth he is the One who will make Bethlehem famous; in Samuel, Kings, and Chronicles he is the one who is King of kings and Lord of lords; in Ezra his is the Temple; In Nehemiah he is the gate into the city; in Esther he is the one who is come to the kingdom for such a time as this; in Job, Jesus is the Redeemer who will stand in the latter day upon this earth. In Psalms, Jesus is the Shepherd; in Proverbs, Jesus is our Wisdom; in Ecclesiastes he is the Creator; in the Song of Solomon he is the One who is indeed our beloved, and in Isaiah he is the Suffering Servant. In Jeremiah he is the righteous branch; in Lamentations he is the One whose compassions and mercies are new every morning; in the Book of Hosea he is the Son who comes out of Egypt; in the Book of Joel he is the name upon whom we call; in the Book of Amos he is the Temple; in Obadiah, Jesus Christ is the Holy One; in Nahum, Jesus is the stronghold in a day of trouble; in Habakkuk Jesus is my strength; in Zephaniah, Jesus is the One to whom all of the meek in the earth come; in Haggai he is the one who tells us to consider our days; in Zechariah he is the King who comes lowly and riding upon a donkey; in Malachi, Jesus is the Son of righteousness who arises with healing in our wings.

Jesus is prophetic truth. He is the Son of God. And so he confronted them with prophetic truth. He also confronted them with historic truth, for the point of this whole overview through the Old Testament was to show them that prophecy had become history, that Jesus Christ, who had been predicted in prophecy, had actually come into human history. You and I are dealing with a Book that is several thousand years old. We pick up a book that was inspired and it gives us a record of historical events that took place centuries before our time. If we are not careful we will have the idea that somehow this is unreal, that somehow this is a fairy tale, that somehow this is mythical, that somehow this is not tangible, literal, actual history. Jesus Christ expounded the Scriptures unto them.

The application that he made of the matter was that all the prophets had written would come to pass had come to pass, and that all the prophets had predicted would happen in the coming of Christ to the cross had taken place, and actually prophecy had become history.

I believe that if at the cross and at the empty tomb they could have set up TV cameras and if it could have been preserved, today we could have shown you a picture of every bit of it happening because I'm dealing with history. I'm dealing with actual facts, and that ought to do something to our hearts. Jesus confronted them with prophetic Scriptures. He confronted them with historic Scriptures, and then he confronted them with dynamic Scriptures.

As Jesus began to deal with the Scriptures it gripped their hearts, and they were never again the same. This Bible will get hold of your heart if you will allow it. The Bible is not like other books. The Bible is God's inspired word. The Bible is God communicating to men in a language which they can understand, and you must not receive the Bible merely as information. Many people have the idea that when they come to church they hear the message as information, and then they go on their way to do like they want. This truth we preach is dynamic truth. If you will allow it to grab your heart it will change your life. If you will somehow take the teachings of the Word of God and let it sink into the deeper recesses of your personality, you will never again be the same. The teachings of the Bible are not intended merely to entertain your intellect or merely intended to arouse your emotion, but the truths of the Word of God are intended to trigger your will and produce change in your life. You ought to be a better person because you hear the Word of God and receive it into your heart. He confronted them with prophetic truth, with historic truth, and with dynamic truth.

But then we also come to the divine *consummation*. It was a seven-mile journey that these disciples made with Jesus, and before they knew it they were already at their place. I think it was the shortest journey they had ever taken. It was short because it was sweet. They were in fellowship with the Lord, and life's journeys get shorter, don't they, when Jesus is with you. Life's journey is smoother when Jesus Christ is walking with you. So they came to their place. Now Jesus put on an act. The Scriptures say that he made as if he would have gone further. He just put on an act to see what they would do, and so the Bible says they invited Jesus into their home. Jesus is a perfect gentlemen. Jesus wants to come into your heart. Jesus wants to rule and to reign as the Lord of your life, but he is a gentlemen. You've got to invite him to come in. In Revelation 3:20 Jesus says, "Behold, I stand at the door and knock: if any man hear my voice and open the door, I will come in to him and sup with him, and he with me." Jesus wants entrance into your heart, but I will knock at the door. Jesus is the light. He is the light of the world. He wants to bring light into your life. Jesus is the king and he wants to rule and to reign over your life. In a picture I saw him knocking at the door, but I had never noticed until sometime ago that there is no latch on the outside of the door. Do you know why? It is because the artist understands properly that when Christ knocks at the door of your heart, the knob is not on the outside. The latch is not on the outside of your heart's door. It's on the inside, and you must open the door. You must ask Jesus Christ to come into your heart and into your life. They "constrained Jesus," that is, they compelled him, they urged him to come into their home. When Jesus came in there was a divine consummation. Jesus Christ sanctified their home. He who had been invited in as the guest became the host, and Jesus took up the bread, broke it, and Jesus gave it to them. The guest became the host, and that is what Jesus does when he comes into a home. Jesus sanctifies that home. Jesus begins to meet the needs of that home. Your home will never be the same if you invite Jesus to come in. He will make a better father out of you. He will make a better mother out of you. He will make a better son or a daughter out of you when you invite him to come and to live. He will sanctify your home, and your home, instead of being a den of demons, can become a little bit of heaven on this earth. It makes a difference when Jesus is in a home.

A few years ago I was visiting one afternoon where I was pastor, and for my first visit I took off across town to a lower-income section where there was a little two-room brick-veneer house. I knocked on the door, and a little voice on the inside said, "come in, preacher. Come in." She knew who it was, and I walked into the little two-room home of Minnie. I wish you could have known Minnie—she was blind, she had terrible arthritis, and her hands were so drawn she couldn't shake with them. Her feet were so drawn she couldn't walk on them, and they had built a little chair on wheels so they could push Minnie around. She was almost bald, and so there she was, bald, blind, but welcoming the preacher. I went in, sat down, and spent about a good half hour with Minnie, and we talked about the goodness of the Lord, and she was just bubbling over and rejoicing about how good Jesus was to her. How sweet life was, how wonderful it was to know the Lord Jesus Christ. In that terrible condition, she was so happy, and I said, "Well, Minnie, I've had a good time. Now I've got to go." She said, "Preacher, before you go we have got to have prayer." So I knelt there on that little linoleum floor, prayed, and said good-bye to Minnie. I left there with warmth in my heart.

I drove across town to one of the elite sections and stopped in front of a magnificent mansion. I walked to the door, knocked, and a maid opened the door and received me into the home. In a little while the lady of the house came and sat down. She was an alcoholic, almost addicted to drugs, and, worst of all, she was lost and needed Jesus. So I began to talk about her need of Jesus, but everything I tried to say she rebutted. She rejected every gospel invitation I made for her to receive Jesus Christ into that magnificent home. She disregarded and spurned Christ. I finally left, and my heart was left cold.

I don't care how magnificent your house may be, or how many antiques may be gathering dust in your home, if Jesus Christ is not a welcome guest in your house, you have a house, not a home. When Jesus comes he sanctifies the home.

When Jesus came into their home he stirred their hearts. Listen to their words in verse 32, "Did not our heart burn within us, while he talked with us by the way, and while he opened to us the scriptures?" As Jesus revealed himself to their hearts as the living Lord, and dealt with the Word of God, their hearts began to be stirred. There is nothing like a heartfelt experience with Jesus Christ. This faith we claim is real and moves the human heart.

I wouldn't give you a nickel for religion you couldn't feel. This is a day of such extreme emotions in religion and many radical groups going around, that there is a danger we will altogether back away from any expression of emotion. We are so afraid of getting out on a limb that we don't even climb the tree! When you really meet the Lord Jesus Christ, it will stir you down to the depths of your being. I'm not advocating foaming at the mouth, and rolling on the floor. I'm simply saying I believe that an experience with Jesus Christ has feeling to it. When I study his Word my heart burns within me.

I think about Jeremiah. Jeremiah was a preacher that became discouraged and decided he was going into the motel business. Jeremiah said, "I made up my mind I wouldn't speak for God anymore. I closed my Bible, and I wouldn't say anything." But do you know what happened to Jeremiah? Jeremiah said, "His word was in mine heart as a burning fire shut up in my bones, and I was weary of forebearing and I could not stay." He had a heartfelt experience with God and couldn't keep it inside of him.

It's a sad day when our churches have gone all the way from the burning heart to the itching ear. It is a tragic time in our churches when we have gone all the way from the amen to the so what? I am amazed at the inconsistencies of people today who claim to love the Lord Jesus Christ. Folks who claim they love Jesus will go to a ball game, and they will shout like Comanche Indians, and then they get to church and sit there like wooden statues. Our churches have become palaces of ice where dull, insipid formality is carried on, nothing gets into the hearts and lives of individuals. I'm talking about heartfelt religion. I'm talking about a heartwarming. This happened to these disciples. The great need of the average Christian today is to have a heartwarming with Jesus Christ.

That will solve the problem of Bible study. You fall in love with the author and have him warm your heart, and you'll want to read about him. That solves the problem of prayer. You have a heartwarming with Jesus, and you won't be able to pray enough. You have a heartwarming with Jesus, and you'll witness—you won't be able to keep your mouth shut. You have a heartwarming, and you won't have any problems about faithfulness to Sunday night services and Wednesday night services. You'll be dead-set to get there. They had a heartwarming. He stirred their hearts.

He sealed their happiness. When they recognized him he disappeared, and they were so excited (v. 33) that they arose the same hour and returned to Jerusalem. They had just been seven miles, and they turned and headed back the same seven miles. I guess you would call that the Jerusalem Marathon. They returned and shared with their fellow-disciples what Jesus had done for them. A dull, dead, emotionless, formal religion never built a church, never sent a missionary, and never won a convert. In These Issues We Must Face, W. A. Criswell told the story about a father who had lost his three-year-old child. Dr. Criswell had the funeral service, and it was a heartbreaking scene. The burial of a little baby is sad, and the little boy's body was there in the casket. At the end of the service the father stood and stared at the dead form of the little boy, and there was no emotion, no evidence of any heartbrokenness. He stood there like a stone statue. Dr. Criswell said he wanted to scream into the ears of the man, "Man, what is wrong with you? Don't you have a heart? Man, can't you at least shed one tear over him? What's wrong with you? Can't you express any emotion over the loss of a little boy?" I think we are like that today when we look at a world that is dead in trespasses and sins, and we stare with no emotion, no compassion. What we need is heartwarming.

Set our souls afire, Lord. Stir us, we pray.

11.
Born Again—From Above

John 3:1-15

The phrase, "born again," is becoming a watchword in our day. Charles Colson, one of the principals in the Watergate scandal, received Jesus Christ as his Savior, and he wrote a best-selling book about it, *Born Again*. In the last two presidental elections, all of the major candidates claimed that they had undergone experiences which they described as "being born again." A Gallup Poll several years ago revealed that one out of every three people interviewed said they had experienced a born-again experience.

What does it mean to be born again? What do people mean when they claim, "I have been born again." What did Jesus mean when he declared to Nicodemus, "Ye must be born again." Born-again is a phrase used to describe an experience which is taught in the New Testament. It is found in several verses in the Word of God. In John 1:12-13, John wrote, "But as many as received him, to them gave he power to become the sons of God, even to them that believe on his name. Which were born, not of blood nor of the will of the flesh nor of the will of man, but of God."

James wrote about being born again in James 1:18, "Of his own will begat he us with the word of truth." In 1 Peter 1:21, "The Rock" wrote, "Being born again, not of corruptible seed, but of incorruptible, by the Word of God that liveth and abideth forever." As you well know, several times in the little book of 1 John, he discusses being born of God, born of the Spirit, born again. This is Bible terminology for the experience we call regeneration, a new birth, a rebirth, a birth from above.

Regeneration is the great need of every person in our world. In fact, Jesus stressed that it is absolutely essential for you to be born again if you are ever going to heaven. People do not need reformation. What they need is regeneration. Reformation is putting a new suit on the old man. Regeneration is putting a new man in the old suit. Reformation is whitewashing; regeneration is washing white. Every generation needs regeneration. Every individual person— every man, every woman, every boy, every girl, and every young person needs the experience which Jesus describes as being born again. The birth experience is most clearly explained in this passage of Scripture, when Jesus talks to Nicodemus, than any other place.

Nicodemus walked upon the stage of Scripture in three different places. He appears here, desiring to talk with the Lord Jesus Christ. He is mentioned again in John 7, where Nicodemus asked the Sanhedrin, "Does our law condemn a man before it hears what he has to say?" There we see him defending the Lord Jesus, and then in John 19, after Jesus had been taken down from the cross, we view his devotion to the Lord Jesus as he brought myrrh, aloes, and spices to anoint the Lord. But this first time when John appears in Scripture, this opening interview with our Lord, tells us exactly what is involved in being born again. As we consider this matter, and as we read about our Lord dealing with Nicodemus, we discover three simple truths about being born again.

One, I call your attention to the must of the new birth. Jesus said in verse 7, "Ye must be born again." Nicodemus came to the Lord by night and made an opening statement which was complimentary and conciliatory to the Lord. He said "Rabbi," and he was making a real concession because Jesus had never been to their school, and for a Pharisee to call Jesus a "Rabbi" was certainly audacious on his part. "We know thou art a teacher come from God, for no man can do these miracles that thou doest, except God be with him." Jesus swept away that opening compliment with a response that must have taken away the breath of Nicodemus. Jesus said, "Verily, verily, I say unto thee, except a man be born again, he cannot see the kingdom of God." Jesus sets before Nicodemus the absolute necessity of the new birth experience.

John Wesley, the founder of the Methodists, was preaching in a location for a period of several weeks. His first message was entitled, "Ye Must Be Born Again." The second time he spoke he used as his subject, "Ye Must Be Born Again." The third time he preached on the same subject. One of the men pulled him aside and said, "Mr. Wesley, I have noticed that every service you have conducted, you have been preaching on the subject of being born again. Mr. Wesley, is that the only Scripture you know? Mr. Wesley, why is it every service you are speaking on that subject?" Mr. Wesley replied, "because, sir, ye must be born again." The new birth is a initial essential, and I think the must of the new birth is revealed in what Jesus said to Nicodemus in verse 3.

First of all it's an absolute necessity to be born again because of the need of humanity. Notice that Jesus said, "Verily, verily, except a man be born again" . . . any person. It was speaking to Nicodemus, but he used the term to involve every person everywhere—"except a man be born again." The need of humanity. We wouldn't expect Jesus to say to a man like Nicodemus, "Ye must be born again." If Jesus had been speaking in a rescue mission somewhere to a bunch of derelicts, then we might understand that they needed to be born again. Or if the Lord had been talking to a group of down-and-outers, we would understand that they needed to be born again. But not a man of the standing of Nicodemus. Nicodemus was quite a prominent man in the city, and yet we are amazed to hear Jesus say to this man, "Nicodemus, ye must be born again."

Now we note three things about Nicodemus as we read these verses, things that make this statement amazing. Number one, I discover that Nicodemus was a rich man. The Bible declares that he was a ruler of the Jews, and this certainly suggests that he was a man of means. There is a tradition which holds that Nicodemus was one of the three richest men in Jerusalem at that time. Others suggest that he was the man who designed the water works for the city of Jerusalem. The fact that he brought a mixture of myrrh and aloes, which was extremely expensive, leads us to believe that this man was *rich,* and yet Jesus ignored all of the riches of Nicodemus and said to him, "Nicodemus, ye must be born again." He was also a *respectable* man. To be a ruler of the Jews meant that he was a member of the Jewish Sanhedrin, The Seventy, a member of the religious supreme court of the Jewish people. He was a prominent man, a respectable leader in his community, and yet Jesus swept away all of his respectability and spoke to him about his need.

And then, of course, we observe, that he was a religious man, for the Bible says that he was a Pharisee. The Pharisees were a group of the set-apart ones, a group of people who believed in the literal interpretation of the Scriptures. He was as fundamental as he was orthodox. He was as religious as one could possibly be, and yet you will also discover that Nicodemus knew nothing about being born again from above.

He should have known something about it. In the Book of Ezekiel there is mention of getting a new heart. The Lord says, "I'll give a new heart unto you. I'll take away that heart of stone, and I will give you a heart of flesh." Nicodemus should have known about the new birth, and yet, with all of his religious learning and for all of his theological training, he had never come to understand that one must be born again. Now he had respect for the Lord Jesus Christ, but he was not yet prepared to receive him as Savior.

He said to the Lord, "Lord, we know you are a teacher come from God." He was wrong in that statement. Jesus Christ was not a teacher come from God. Jesus Christ was God come down to teach. For all his religion Nicodemus needed to be born again. To this kind of man we probably would have said, "How about moving your letter?" but Jesus said to him, "Ye must be born again." I am amazed as I read the New Testament at how many respectable, religious people were converted by the power of Jesus Christ. There was Paul of Tarsus, the religious leader of his time, and yet he had to be born again. There was the rich young ruler who came to the Lord Jesus Christ and Jesus talked to him about a heart-changing experience. It ought to be a warning to all of us not to assume anything. This ought to be a warning for us not to rest upon our religious affiliation. It ought to warn us not to depend on our church membership or our religion. Jesus' statement could be made to all humanity, for this is the need of humanity.

The Bible states that all have sinned and come short of the glory of God. When Adam sinned in the Garden of Eden he passed to the whole human race the seeds of sin, the heredity of a sinful nature. In Psalm 51 David wrote, "Behold, I was shapen in iniquity, and in sin did my mother conceive me." He was not saying that the act of conception is sin, but that we were born with a sinful nature, and that is why, my friends, you must be born again. You were born wrong the first time, and so you need a second birth. You need a birth from above that will change you in the heart and in the core of your being.

But Jesus also said, "Ye must be born again" because of the *nature* of *heaven*. Now Jesus said here in verse 3, "Except you are born again you cannot see the kingdom of God." The word again there is the Greek word which may mean "from above." You must be born, Jesus says, "from above." A spiritual birth. You have had your physical birth, you have had your fleshly birth, but in order to see heaven you must receive a birth from above. This is what Peter meant in his first epistle when he talked about being "a partaker of the divine nature." In other words, before you can get into heaven, heaven has got to get into you. You wouldn't fit into heaven in your natural condition. You'd be totally out of place if you went to heaven without being born again. You would be miserable up there, for there has to be a change in your nature.

Why, you take a fish and put that fish in the air, and it doesn't fare well because it is not the nature of a fish to live in the air. Or you take a bird and bury that bird in an underground cave, and it won't do so well because it is contrary to the nature of a bird to live below the ground. And you will never see a pig teaching astronomy, nor will you ever see a snail building a house. Do you know why? It's simply not their nature to do that, and the same is true of a human being apart from the new birth. Heaven is a prepared place for a prepared people. God has to do a new work in your life; your heart has to be changed; you have to receive a birth from above if you are going to heaven.

That was not a suggestion, a hint, or a gentle reminder, Jesus laid it down as an outright necessity. You *must* be born again. Two, Jesus also talks about the mystery of the new birth. Jesus immediately got the attention of Nicodemus. Nicolemus was probably an old man. I had never realized that until I studied this Scripture, but if you will look at what he says in verse 4 you will certainly get that idea. Nicodemus asked, "How can a man be born when he is old?" I think Nicodemus was saying, "Young rabbi, young teacher, I am an old man. What you have suggested is interesting indeed. I am concerned about it. Oh, that I could start over again." I think all us kind of feel like Nicodemus must have felt. I don't know about you, but there have been times along the way I wished I could have started over. Have you ever wished you could be just a little boy or a little girl again and live through your life?

· You remark, "Oh, preacher, if I could just start over again, I would do a lot of things differently. I would change some decisions I have made." I think Nicodemus was thrilled with the prospect. But he was puzzled about the possibility, and so he queried Jesus, "How, how can a man be born when he is old? Can he enter the second time into his mother's womb and be born?" He was puzzled by the mystery of the new birth. There is a mystery to it, and quite frankly I am glad there is a mystery to the new birth. I am glad there are areas of my Christian life that are beyond my ability to understand, I am glad I have a book, the Bible, that has mystery in it. I'm glad I have a God who is the God of mystery. I can't understand all there is to know about it, and I am glad that what God has done for me in the person of the Lord Jesus has mysteries that are deeper than my ability to understand. If I could understand it all, if you took all of the mystery out of it, then I would question whether or not it was of a supernatural, divine God. There are some mysteries about it.

Friend, the mystery of the new birth ought not to cause you to miss out on it. Simply because you don't understand something is no reason for you to miss it or fail to enjoy it. There are many things we don't understand in life. An unbelieving professor once remarked to his students, "Young men, I advise you never to believe anything you can't understand." I can't think of a more stupid statement. What did you mean, "Never accept anything you can't understand"? There is much we don't understand, and yet we accept. I don't understand the mystery of electricity. You may understand why some things happen about it, but there are other areas of electricity beyond the grasp of man. There is a mystery about electricity. I don't understand how there is a power supply somewhere that generates an electrical current and brings it into our churches and homes. I believe in it enough that I don't put my thumbs in any light sockets anywhere! I accept electricity, but there is a mystery about it. Can you imagine a man in the fifth story of a burning hotel, and the firemen come with a canopy, and they yell, "Jump, jump, you are going to burn to death!" He replies, "I'm not jumping until you explain to me how the fire started, and I won't jump until you can tell me the physical constitution of that canopy, how it is put together, and tell me something about the firemen and explain the whole process to me." Listen, if you are in a burning building it doesn't matter how it started; it doesn't matter how you are going to get rescued. The simple and sane action is to jump and be rescued, and I don't understand how God would love me enough to save me.

I don't understand the mystery of the new birth, how God brings it about, but I have experienced it, and I enjoy the benefit and the blessings of the experience. So can you, and so Jesus talked about the mystery of it.

In order to help us understand the mystery he uses two figures of speech about things we do not understand. First of all, he taught that the new birth is like a birth, like physical birth. There is tremendous debate about this fifth verse. People wonder what it means when Jesus said, "Except a man be born of water. . . . " And some think it means the Word of God. And it may. Sometimes I seem to feel that when John refers to water he is talking about the Word of God, but I really believe that Jesus here had in mind a physical birth. Medical doctors indicate that physical birth is heavily involved with water. In the next verse Jesus made it even clearer (verse 6): that which is born of flesh is flesh, the physical birth, and that which is born of the Spririt is spirit, the spiritual birth. Being born again can be compared to the experience of physical birth.

Let's compare the two for a moment. Number one, *birth brings life.* When a birth takes place life begins in this world. Golf balls don't have life because they are manufactured: they are not born. They don't have life because they have never experienced birth, but babies have life because babies are born. And that's what it means to be born spiritually. It means that you receive a life you did not have. Why, here is a person who has no interest in the things of God, no eyes to see spiritual truths, no heart to feel spiritual depths, and then one day he has a born-again experience. One day he receives the Lord Jesus into his heart, and do you know what takes place? Birth and life begin to pulsate through his being.

John wrote in his first epistle (5:12): "He that hath the Son hath life, and he that hath not the Son of God hath not life." Birth produces life. Birth involves two parents, a mother and a father. The spiritual birth involves the Word of God and the Spirit of God. First Peter 1:23 says, "Being born again, not of corruptible seed, but of incorruptible, by the Word of God that liveth and abideth forever." The Spirit of God takes the Word of God and produces a child of God. When the Word of God is preached, that Word goes down into the heart of a lost sinner. It impregnates that heart, so to speak, and the Spirit of God begins to convict. The Spirit of God takes the Word of God, and when that lost sinner repents of sin and invites the Lord Jesus into his heart, he is born again by the Word of God and by the Spirit of God.

Birth is never repeated. If I asked you, talking in physical terms, "How many times have you been born?" you would look at me, scratch your head, and probably say, "Listen, man, did you just come from the funny farm?" You are born only one time. And we know that is true—physical birth takes place one time, and the same thing is true spiritually. The spiritual birth occurs one time. It's a once-for-all experience. Jesus didn't say to Nicodemus, "You must be born again and again and again and again and again." The moment you are born into the family of Jesus Christ you receive new life from him. You become a member of God's family, and you are a member for all time and all eternity. Birth is a no repeat experience.

Birth is a definite experience as well. There is a definite moment when birth occurs. The doctor spanks a baby, it cries, and life begins. There was a period of preparation building up to that birth but there has to be a definite time. When I talk to people about being saved, I can nearly always tell if they aren't by this kind of response. "Oh, yes, I'm saved." I answer, "That's great. Tell me about it." "Oh, I have always been a Christian." Immediately I know they have never been saved because there is a definite time. There may have been months of preparation, days when the Spirit of God used the Word and dealt with your heart. There my have been times when friends witnessed to you, months when the songs and the sermons began to make their impact on your heart, but somewhere, at some point in time, there must be a definite experience—when you pass from death unto life and are born definitely and decisively into the family of God.

Being born again is like physical birth. It's like physical birth in that there is pain involved. Every mother must endure pain in order to "birth" a child. That mother must go literally through "the valley of the shadow of death" in order for life to be brought forth. The same is true in your spiritual birth. There had to be pain for you to be born, and Jesus went to the cross of Calvary and shed his blood. His hands, feet, and side were torn and wounded. And Jesus suffered like no other person ever suffered to make it possible for you to be born into the family of God.

It took an infinite price, an infinite cross for Jesus to die for your sins. It's like birth. If you have been born only once, you will die two times, but if you have been born two times you will die only one time. You must be born again.

I heard about an old gentleman who woke up one morning and, much to his dismay and alarm, he read his name in the obituary column. That shook him up, he got on the phone, and called the editor of that newspaper. The editor realized that there had been an error, and he replied, "Cheer up, old man, we'll put your name in the birth column in the morning and give you a fresh start." That 's exactly what the new birth does. The new birth puts your name into the birth column. Your name is written down in the Lamb's Book of Life. You are born into the family of God. You ask, "How can that be?" I don't understand it. It's a mystery, but you don't have to understand birth in order to experience it.

It's also like the breeze. I think about that time Nicodemus maybe felt the gentle breeze blow across his face, perhaps heard the breeze as it blew through the narrow streets of the city where they talked, and then Jesus reached once again into the world of nature and illustrated the mystery of the new birth. "Nicodemus, Nicodemus, the wind blows where it wants to. You can hear the sound thereof but you can't tell where it came from. You don't know where it is going." There is a mystery about the wind. I feel sorry for our weathermen. They have a difficult time trying to predict the weather. Did you hear about the weatherman who left town because the weather didn't agree with him? I can certainly understand how that must be.

I heard about a gentleman standing with a rope, and a fellow came by and inquired, "Old man, what is that?" The old man answered, "That's a weather gauge. When the rope is moving the wind is blowing, and when the rope is wet it is raining." There is a mystery about that wind. You can't tie a rope to the wind, you can't catch the wind in a basket, you can't lock the wind up in a jail somewhere. The wind blows where it wants to. You can't see the wind, but you can feel the wind, and you can see the effects of it. We can view the effects of the wind, and we can see in the spiritual realm the effects of the new birth.

You don't have to understand it to know the change in the life of an individual who has been born of the Spirit of God. Look at Charles Colson. I have heard that man as he preached and gave his testimony for the Lord. Who can question the change in the life of this man? Over and over again we see the effects and the changes in the lives of human beings because they have experienced being born again of the Spirit of God. So Jesus talked about the must of the new birth, the mystery of the new birth, and the meaning of the new birth.

Nicodemus came back with a question in verse 9, "How can these things be?" He was no longer doubting the possibility of it, but the methodology of it. How does this come about? What does it mean? what causes it to happen? What makes it possible for the new birth to occur? Jesus in verse 10 queried, "Art thou a master of Israel, and knowest not these things?" In Greek the definite article is used here, "Art thou *the* teacher of Israel?" Listen to that. Nicodemus was one of the greatest teachers of his time. In that day he might have been the greatest preacher of the Jewish people. Here was a preacher who needed to be saved. Here was a theologian, a scholar that needed to be saved. Don't ever presume on your religious affiliation, my friend. Don't assume because you are teaching Sunday School or singing in the choir or serving as a deacon that everything is all right between you and Jesus.

You would be surprised how many religious folks don't know that we must be born again. You would be surprised how many people are sitting in churches and thinking that everything is OK, and if they died, that moment they would go to hell. Some of you may be in that situation right now, feeling comfortable and at ease in your religion, and yet you have never understood that it is absolutely essential, you must be born again.

Jesus said (verse 11): "Verily, verily. . . ." That is the third time Jesus said, "Verily, verily." Did you notice that? He said it back in verses 3 and 5. Everytime I read that I think about a preacher I had on radio many years ago. People would write in questions for that preacher to answer, and his wife would read the question to him— then he would answer. On a particular broadcast someone had written in about "verily, verily." His wife read the question: "Dear Bishop: What does it mean when the Bible says, *verily, verily?*" The Bishop answered, "Well, verily, verily is a very important word in the Scriptures. In fact, verily, verily is such an important word that when Jesus verilys, he doesn't verily once—he verilys twice. Next question."

The word *verily* is close to the word *amen.* When Jesus uses that word you had better perk up your ears. He has something to say that is extremely important. Jesus, talking about the means of the new birth, said, "Verily, verily. I've told you earthly things, and you don't understand them. How will you understand if I tell you heavenly things?" Then Jesus proceeded to tell him of heavenly things.

And he showed Nicodemus the two parts necessary in order for the new birth. First of all, he showed us the Savior's part (verses 13 and 14): "No man ascended up to heaven, but he that came down from heaven, even the Son of man which is in heaven." He was talking about His coming into this world. The new birth is possible because Jesus came into this world. You can be saved today, you can be born into the family of God because Jesus was willing to leave heaven and come down. This world has experienced a visit from outer space. A visitor from another world came here two thousand years ago, and his name was Jesus. Ah, what a trip it was. Down from his glory the great Creator came, and Jesus was his name. Jesus the Savior walked on this earth. Then he declared in verse 14: "As Moses lifted up the serpent in the wilderness, even so must the Son of man be lifted up"—and that is the second *must* in the passage. In verse 7 he said to Nicodemus the sinner, "Ye must be born again." That is the sinner's must, but now here is the Savior's must. The Son of man must be lifted up. He was talking about the must of the cross.

In John 12:32 Jesus said, "And I, if I be lifted up from the earth, will draw all men unto me." Jesus was lifted up on that cross in order to make it possible for you to be born again. Jesus gave an illustration of his cross taken from the Old Testament picture book. He told the story of the Israelites who had been bitten by the fiery serpents, and they were dying from the poison of those serpents. They came to Moses and cried, "Moses, do something for us!" Moses prayed to the Lord and the Lord said, "Moses, you take a serpent made of brass, put it on a pole, and tell the people if they will look at that uplifted serpent they will be healed."

Moses put a serpent on the pole and I guess some of them said, "Why, Moses, what are you putting a serpent on that pole for? They are our trouble." That was a picture of why Jesus went to the cross. The Bible teaches that when Jesus was lifted up on the cross that God "made him who knew no sin to be sin for us." Jesus was lifted up for our sins. Our sins nailed him to the cross. When Jesus died on that cross he did something to make it possible for us to be saved. That was the Savior's part. He has already done his part.

But now here is the sinner's part (verse 15)—"Whosoever believeth in him should not perish but have eternal life." I'm glad he didn't put my name in that verse. I'm glad that he didn't say that if Jerry Vines believed in him he would have eternal life. I've met two people in my lifetime who have the same name as I, and if he had put Jerry Vines in the verse, there would be some doubt about which Jerry Vines. In order that I might not misunderstand, and know that it is for me too, the Lord simply used the word *who-*

soever. Do you know who that means? That means me, that means you, that means anybody who wants to. The Scriptures' invitation is "whosoever will, let him come." The only requirement necessary for you to be born again is to *want* to be born again. If you will believe on him you will have everlasting eternal life. "Ye must be born again!"